BUILT BY LOVING HANDS
The Barn Photography of Marilyn Brummet

Built By Loving Hands: The Barn Photography of Marilyn Brummet
Copyright © 2019 by Aaron Brummet
Published by Aaron Brummet
Designed by Seth Hammond
First Printing: 2019
ISBN: 978-1-79-089057-6

BUILT BY LOVING HANDS

The Barn Photography of Marilyn Brummet

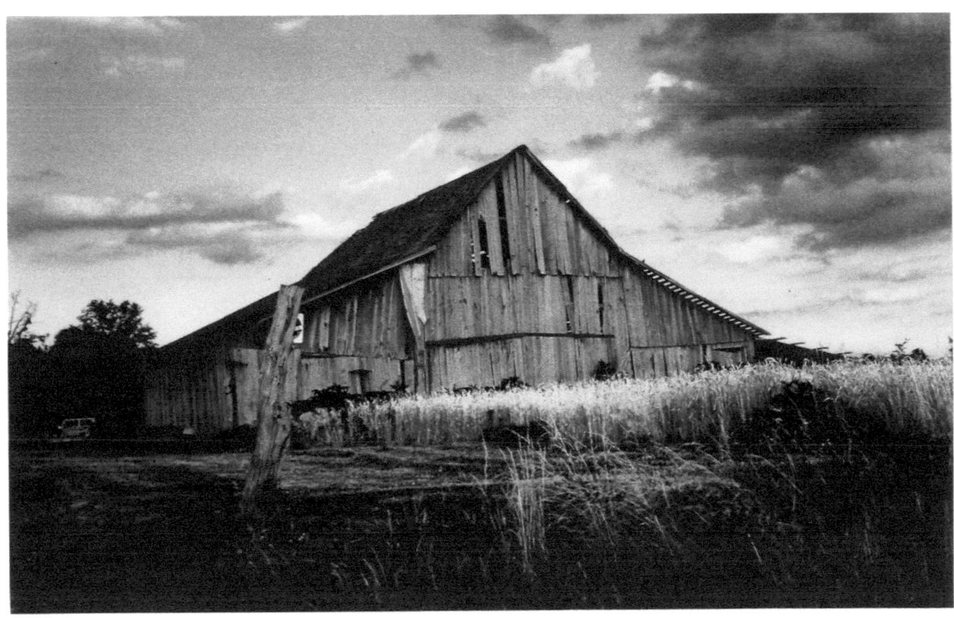

Written by Aaron Brummet

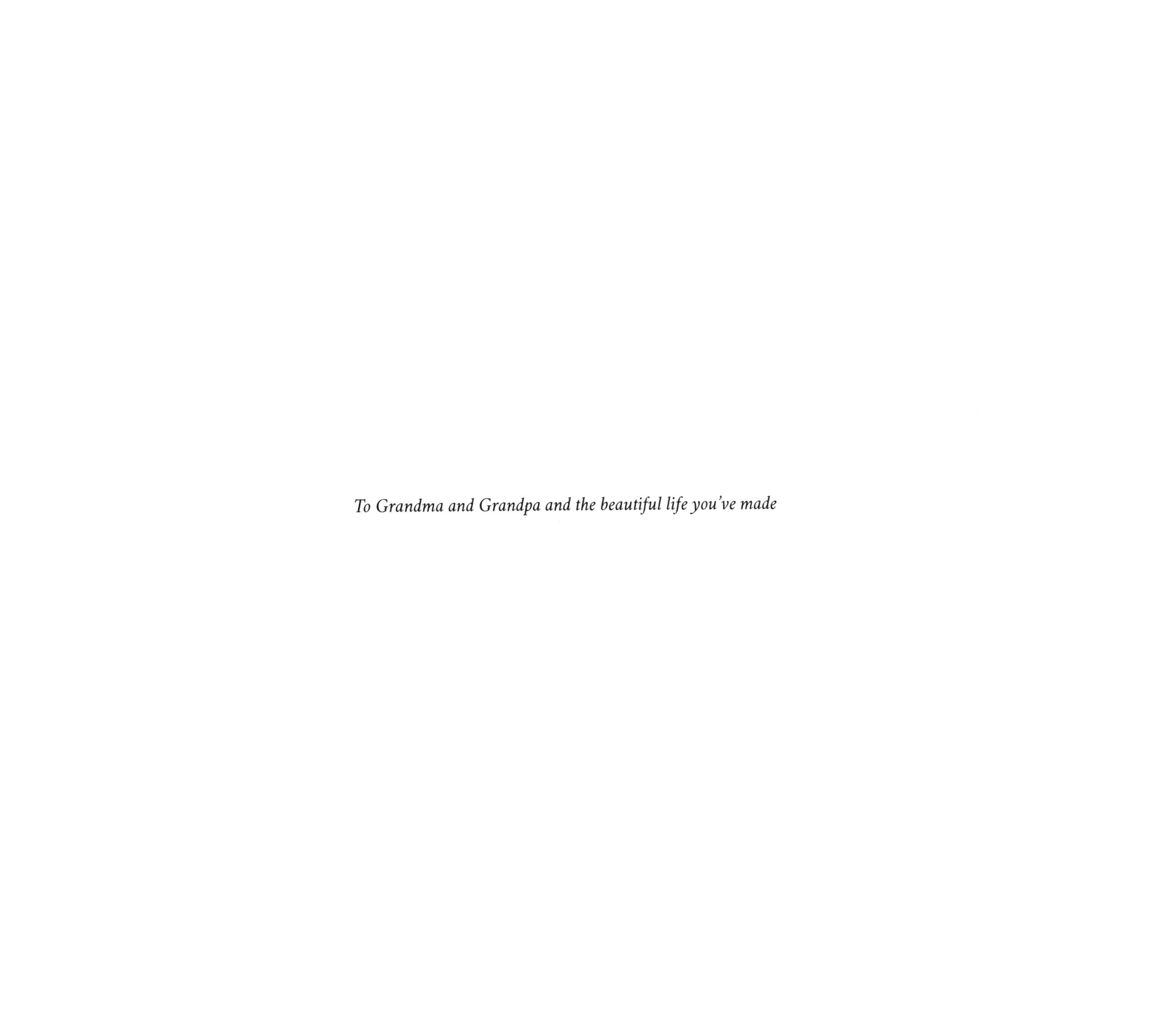

To Grandma and Grandpa and the beautiful life you've made

Marilyn Brummet was a woman of quiet work. She spent most of her life as a wife, a mother, a grandmother, and a nurse. She adored nature. She could identify every bird that visited the numerous feeders and houses she set up. And her applesauce was unmatched in the history of applesauces. But it was only after she departed that I learned just how much of herself she'd given to another passion: photography. In looking through the physical possessions she left behind, I discovered over 1,300 photographs of barns, taken over a 30-year span and compiled into at least six full albums and a shoebox. She took photos of other things she loved as well, such as her family, her travels, and the fascinating plants and animals she encountered. But it was the barns that stood out to me. Each one was uniquely designed for its purpose. Some looked clean and functional. Others had been overcome by weather and wildlife to the point of being barely recognizable as barns. But most were somewhere in between. These seemed to be her favorites. The ones that didn't quite resemble their first forms, but retained every bit of their original beauty. I have a hunch that, to her, this might have made them even more beautiful. My grandmother saw beauty in creation and the life around her.

I hope here to show a snapshot of the beauty in the life she made.

–Aaron Brummet

I am built by loving hands

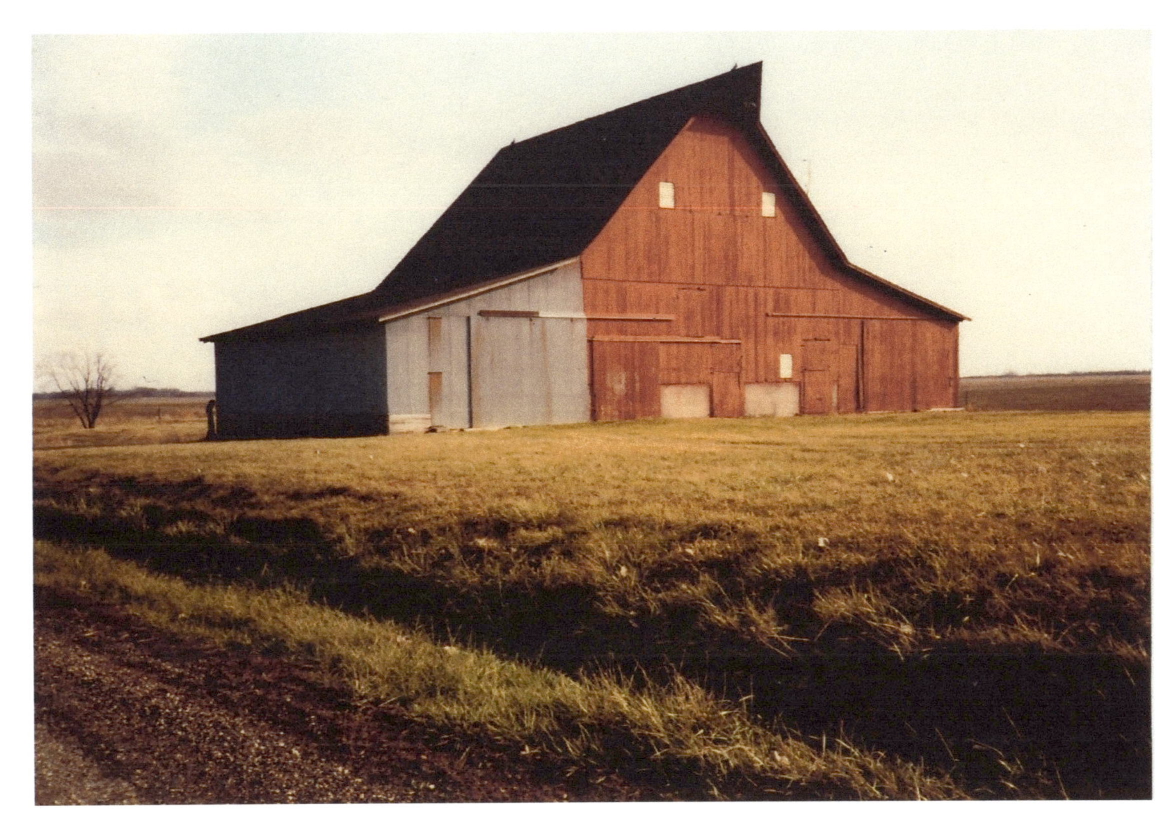

Barn on rd. south of here.
Dec '84

Marilyn Brummet
O.B. Dept.

To be enlarged

Designed by a master craftsman

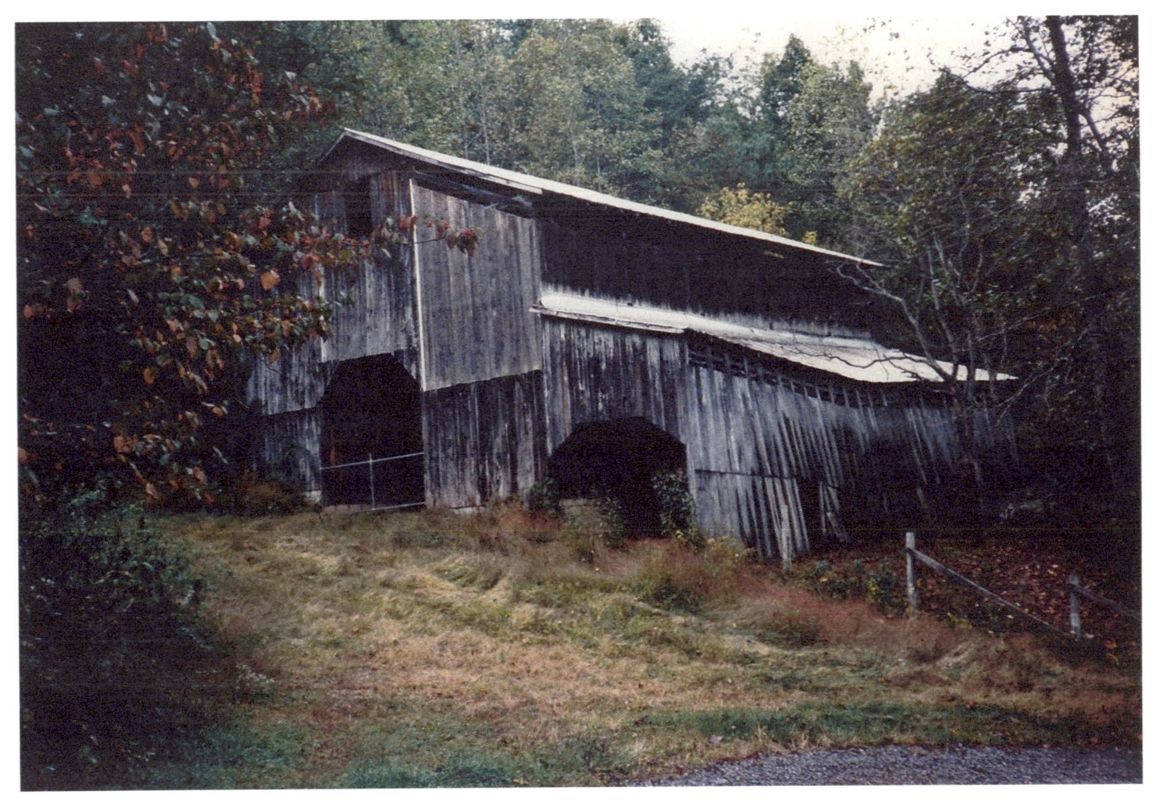

Near
Hattinburg, Tenn.

Based on a perfect blueprint

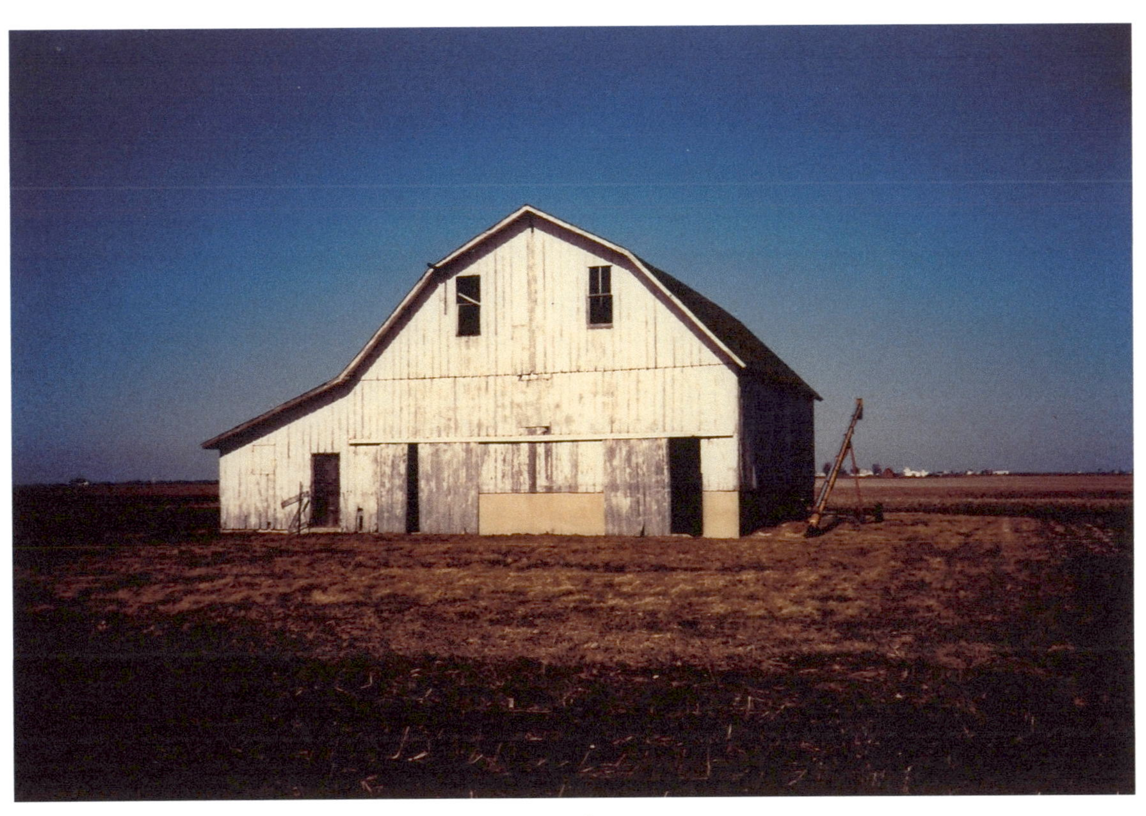

Bratt barn
March '85

A carpenter's labor of love

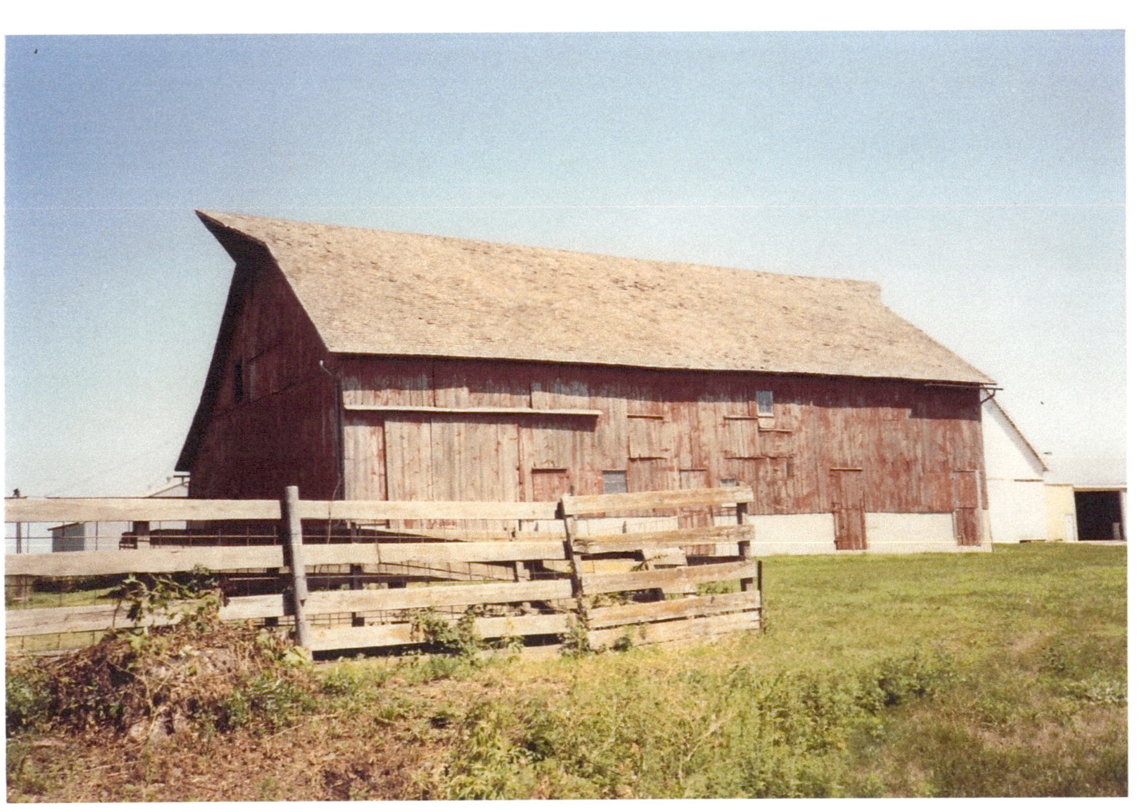

I am stable, sturdy, and secure

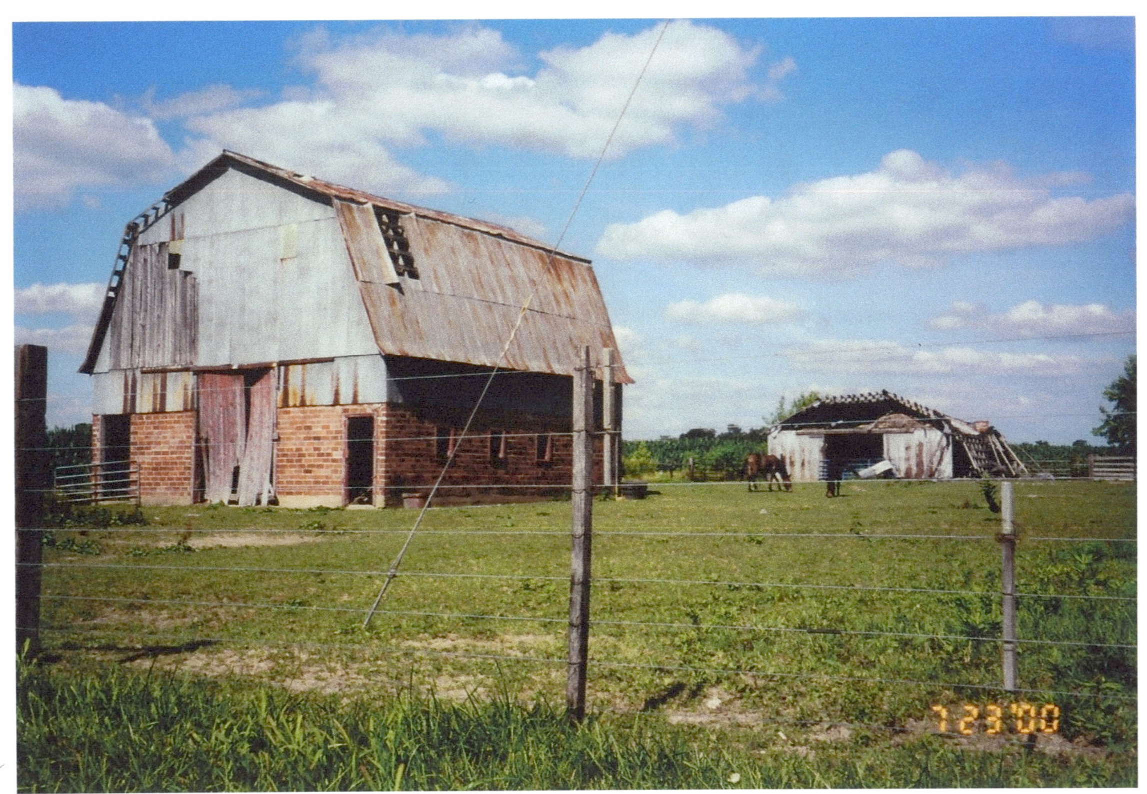

Dear
Arthur

Put together with a purpose

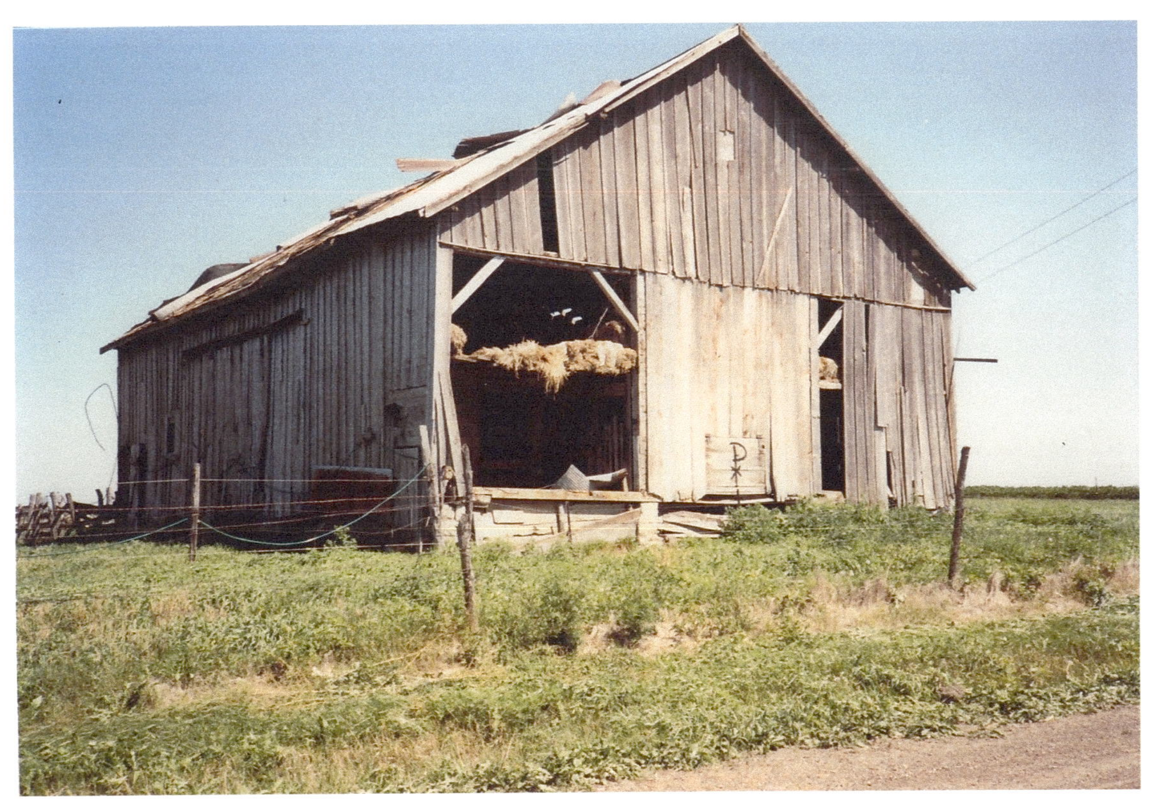

Every element in place

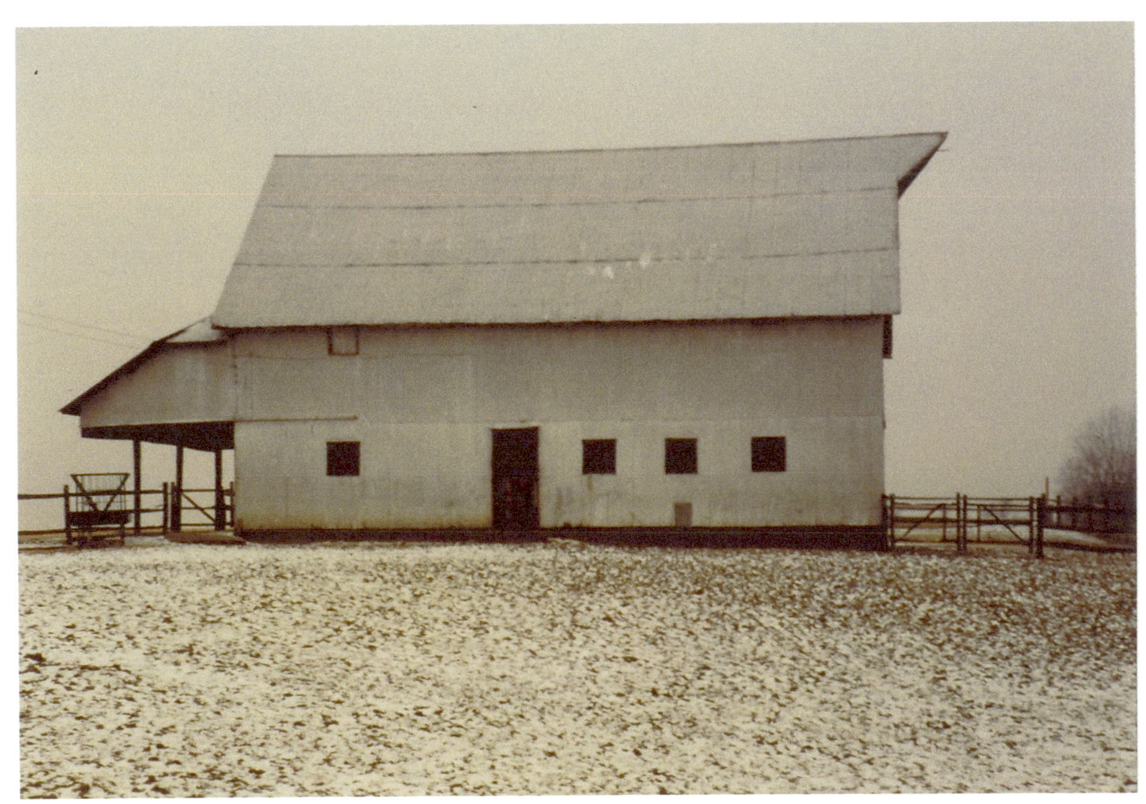

Without a detail left to chance

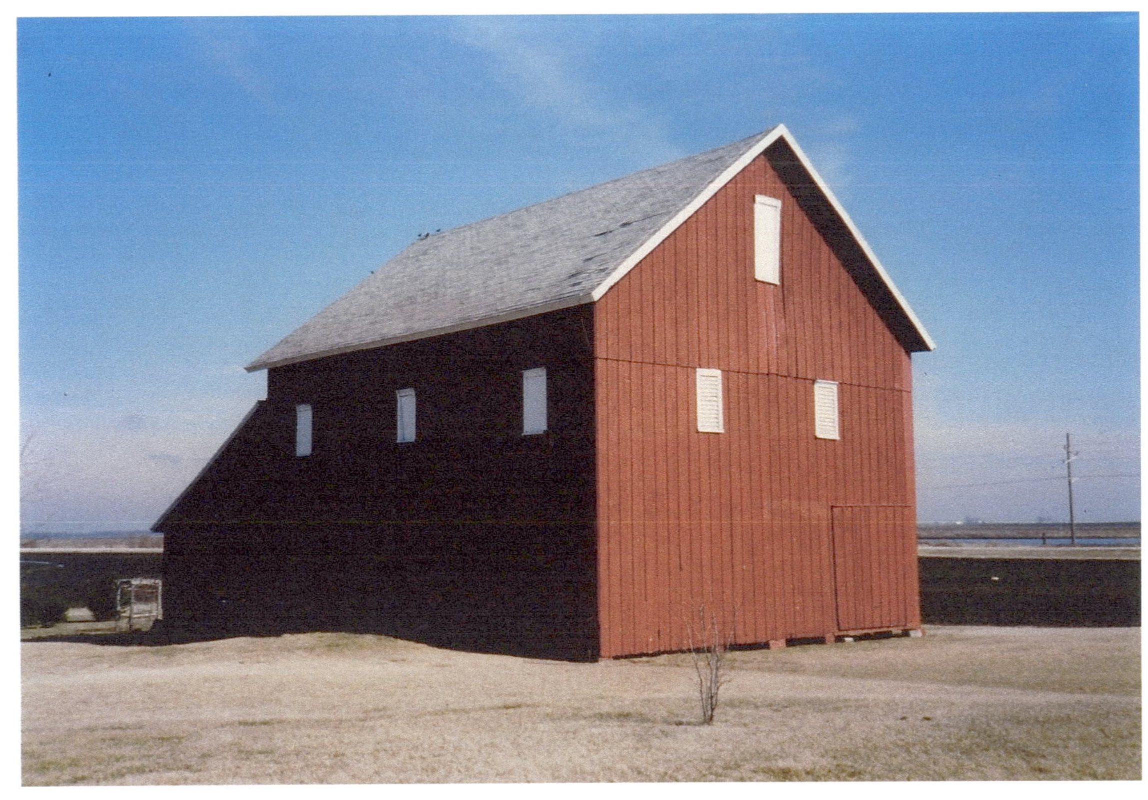

March 1997
Feb 97

I am given to my work

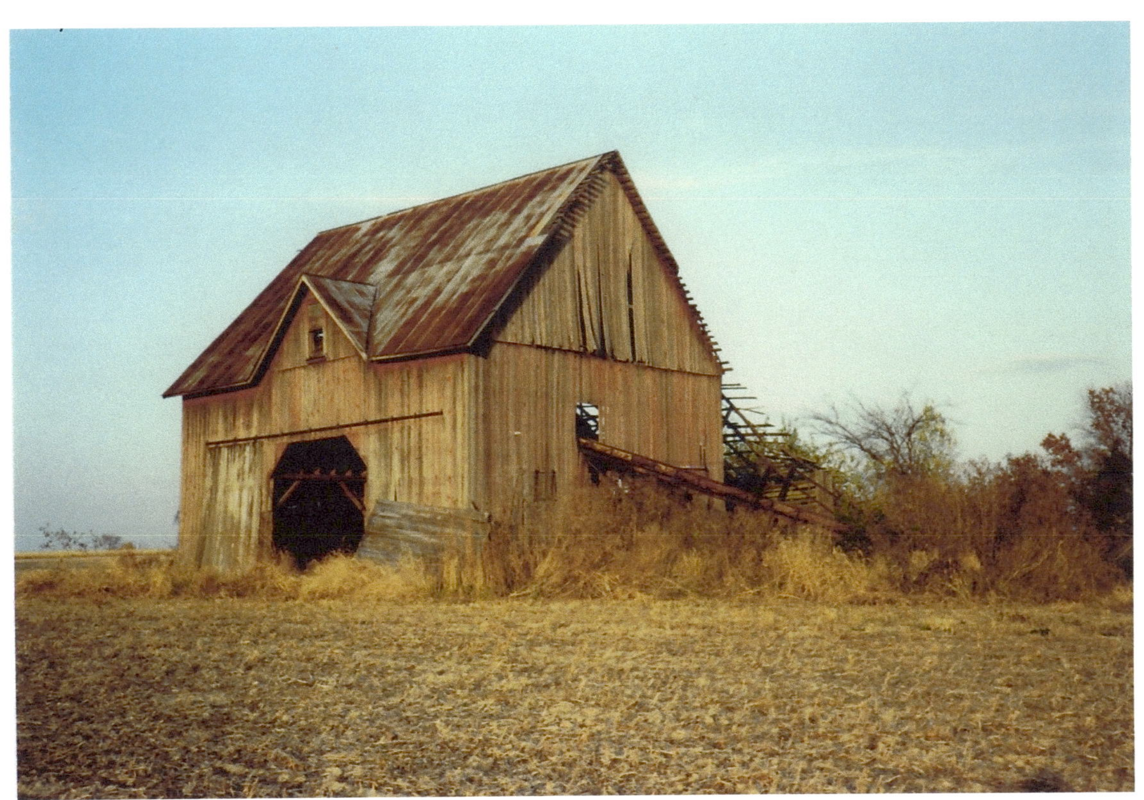

West of
Mattoon

Which was with me from the start

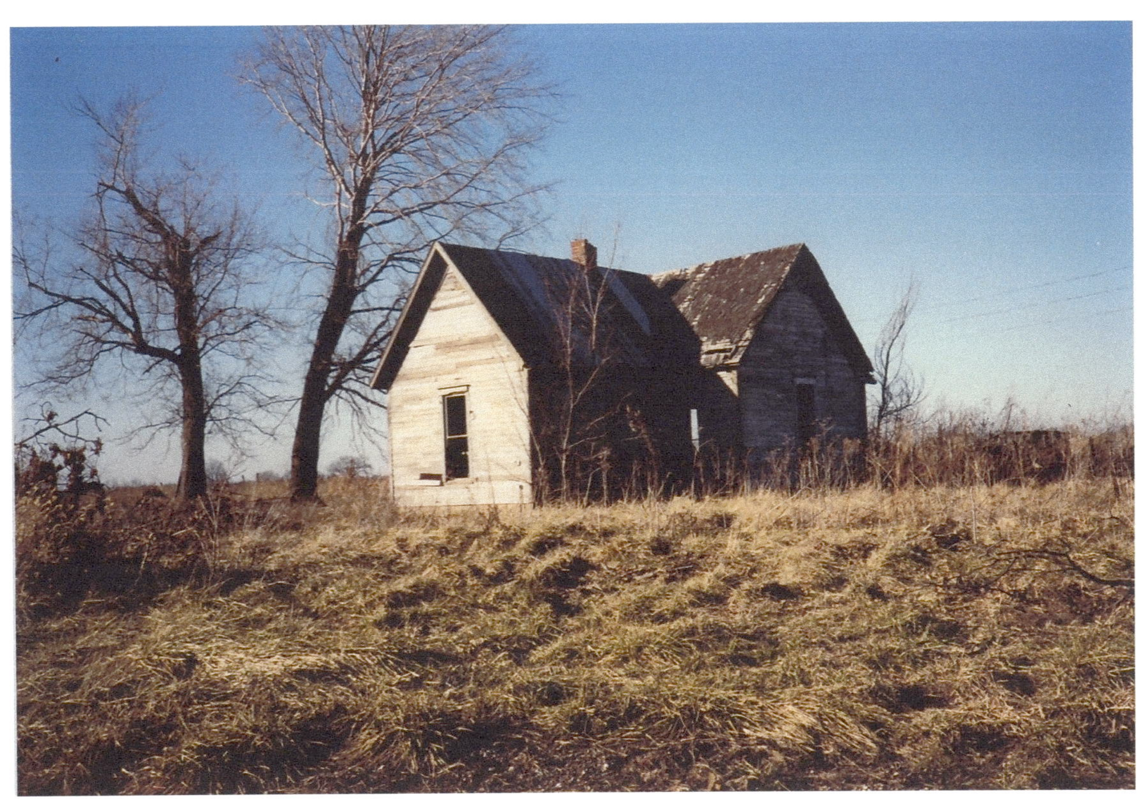

Along with every tool

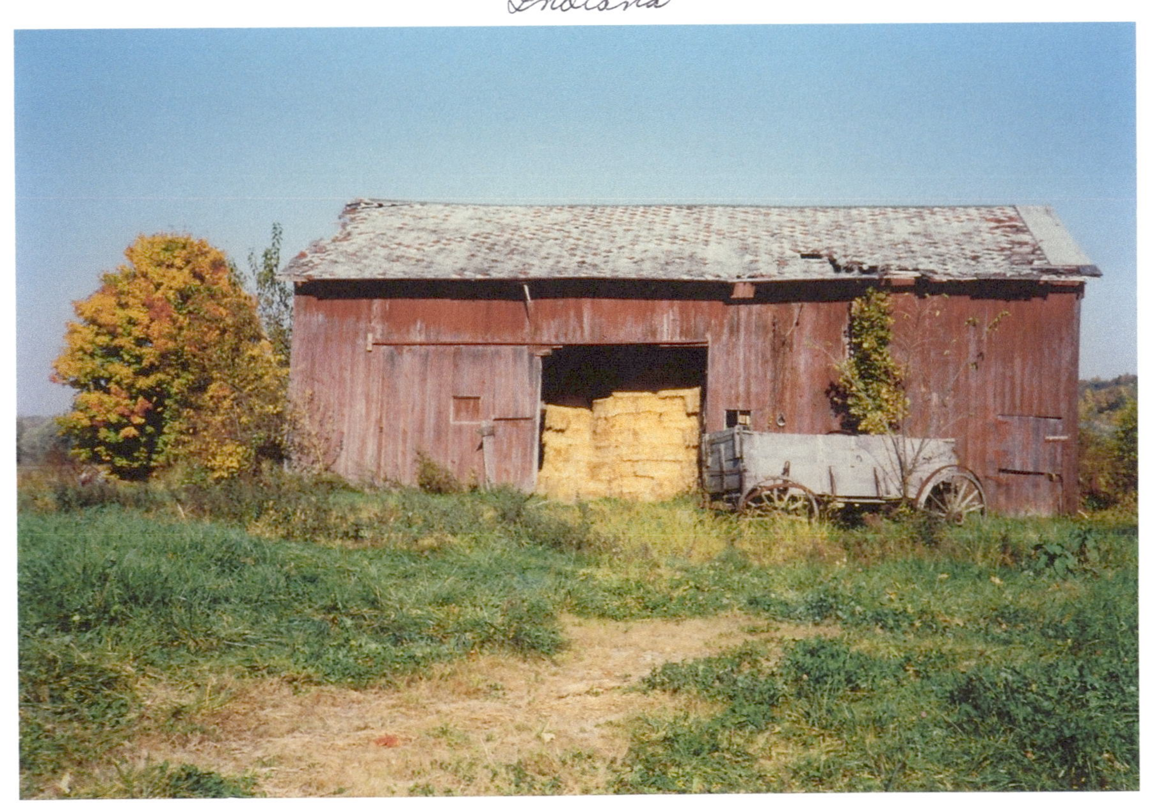

Indiana

That would help me see it through

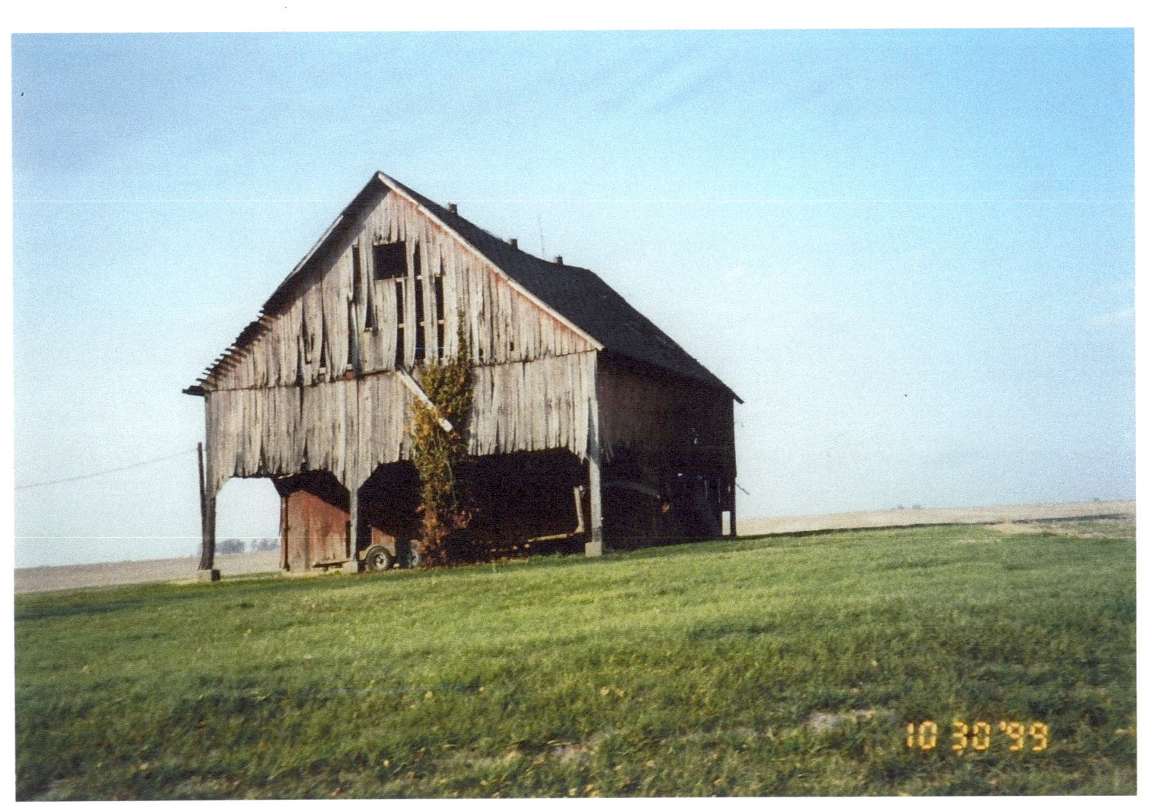

On Way home from
Turkey Run, Ind.

I am unique among many

Cantilever Barn
Cades Cove Rd
Gatinburg Tenn

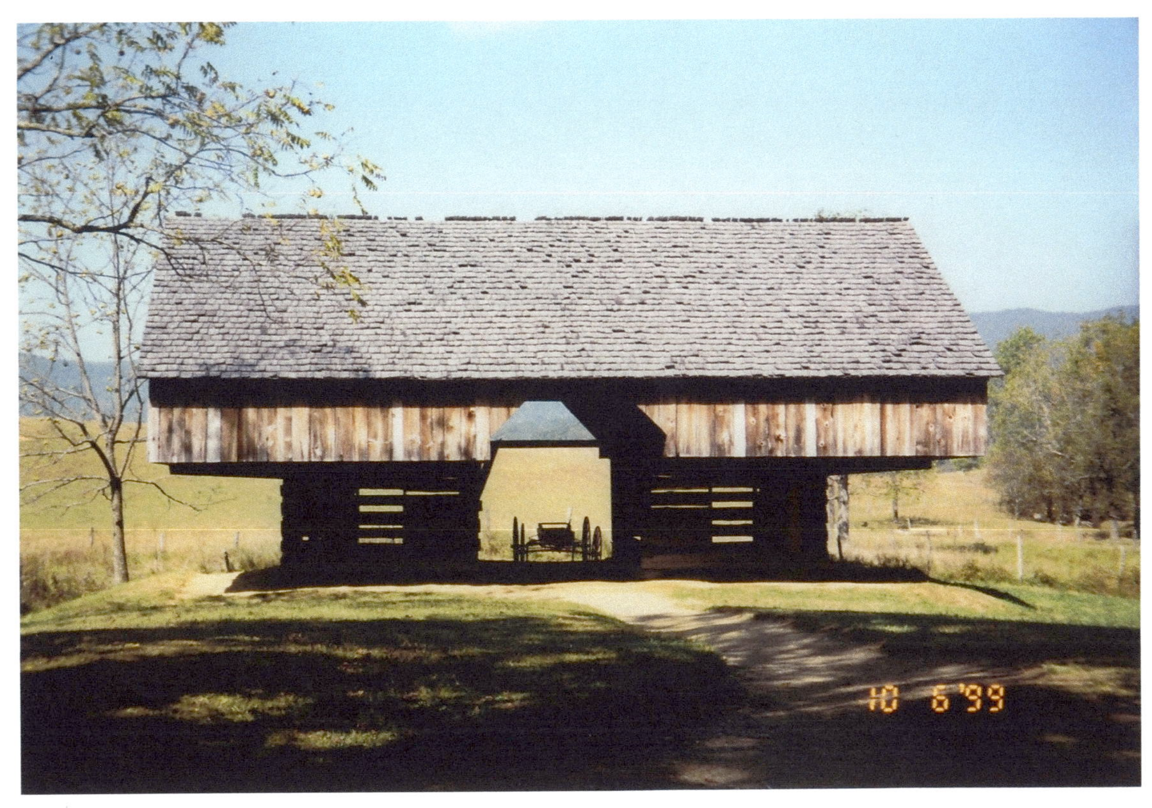

Arriving in an era

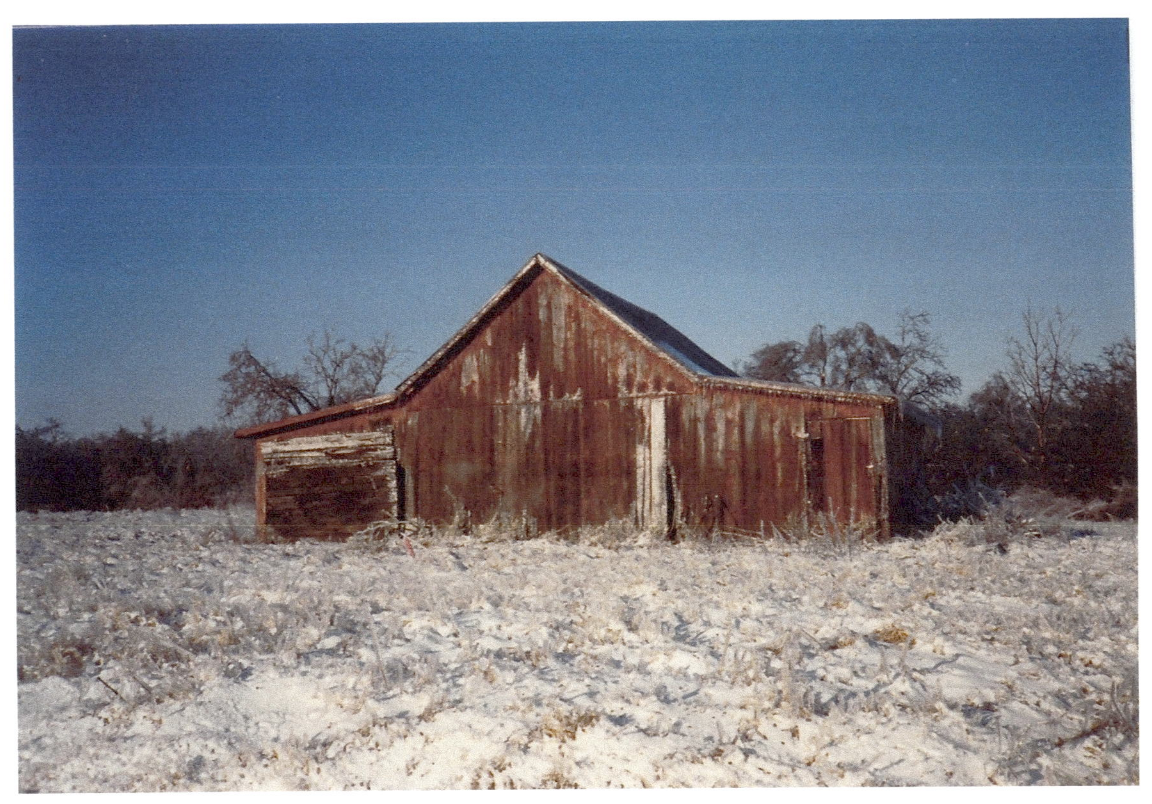

Barn on Lerna Road
March '88

Placed with precision

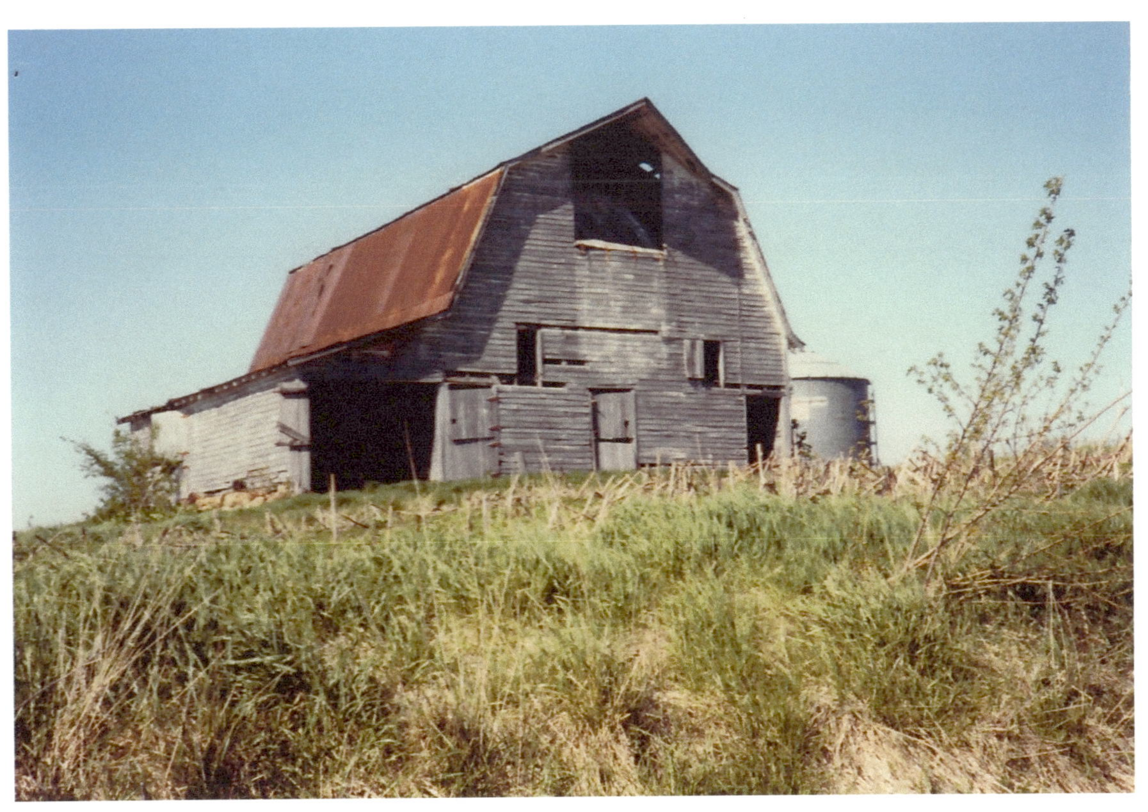

Exactly in my role

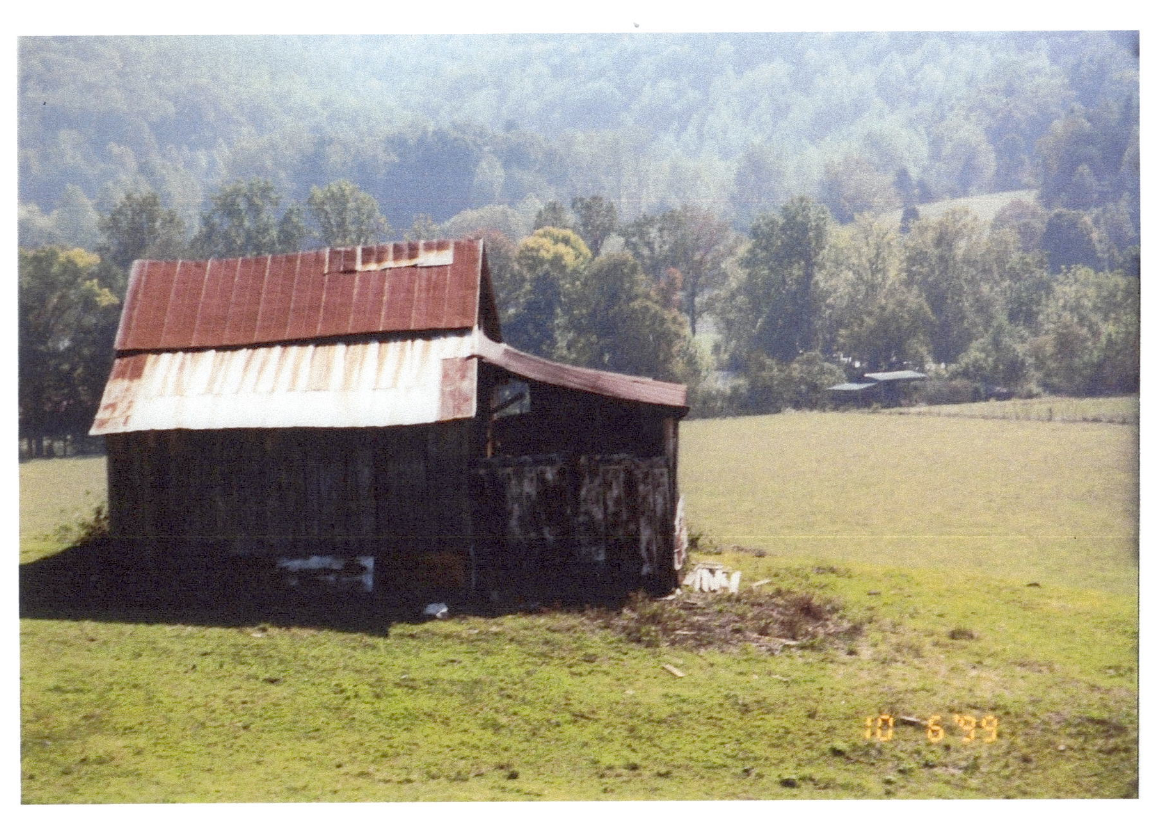

Cades Cove Rd
Gattenburg, Tenn

I am full of love

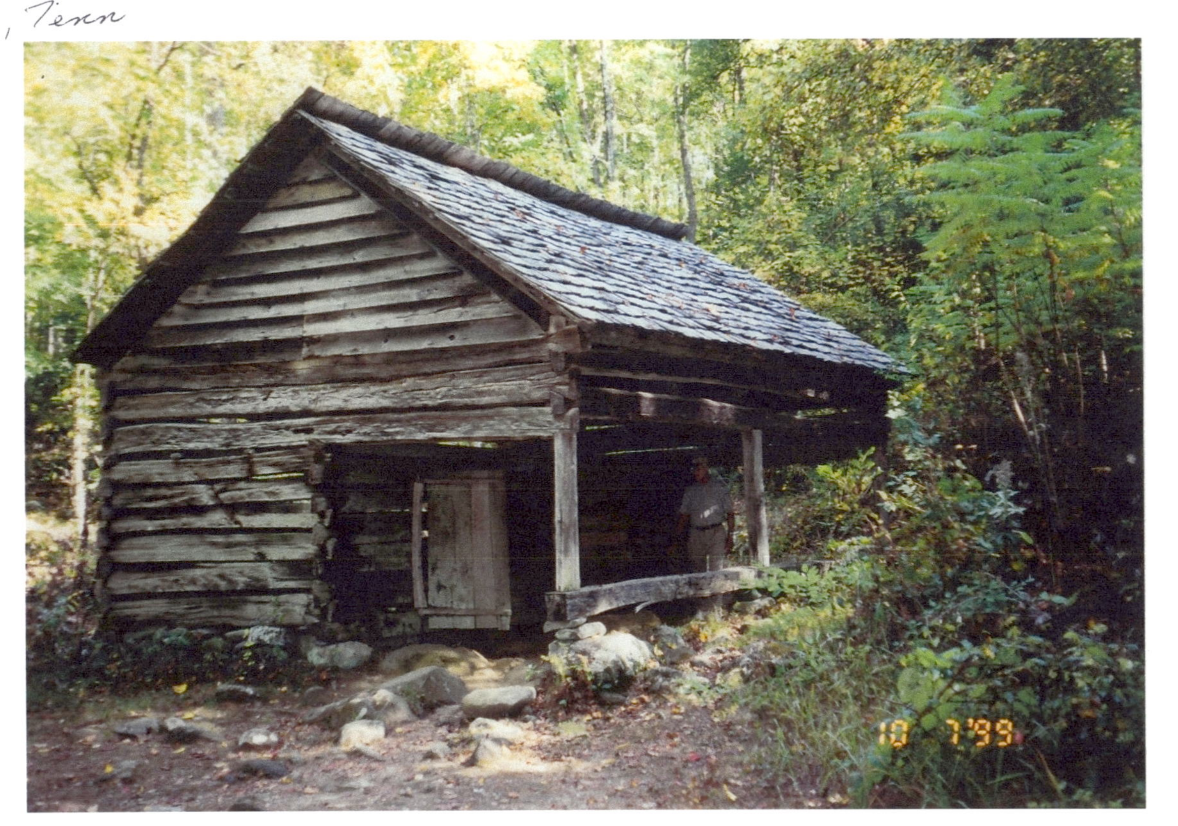
Roaring Fork Motor Trail
Gatlinburg, Tenn

Oft imperfect or unkempt

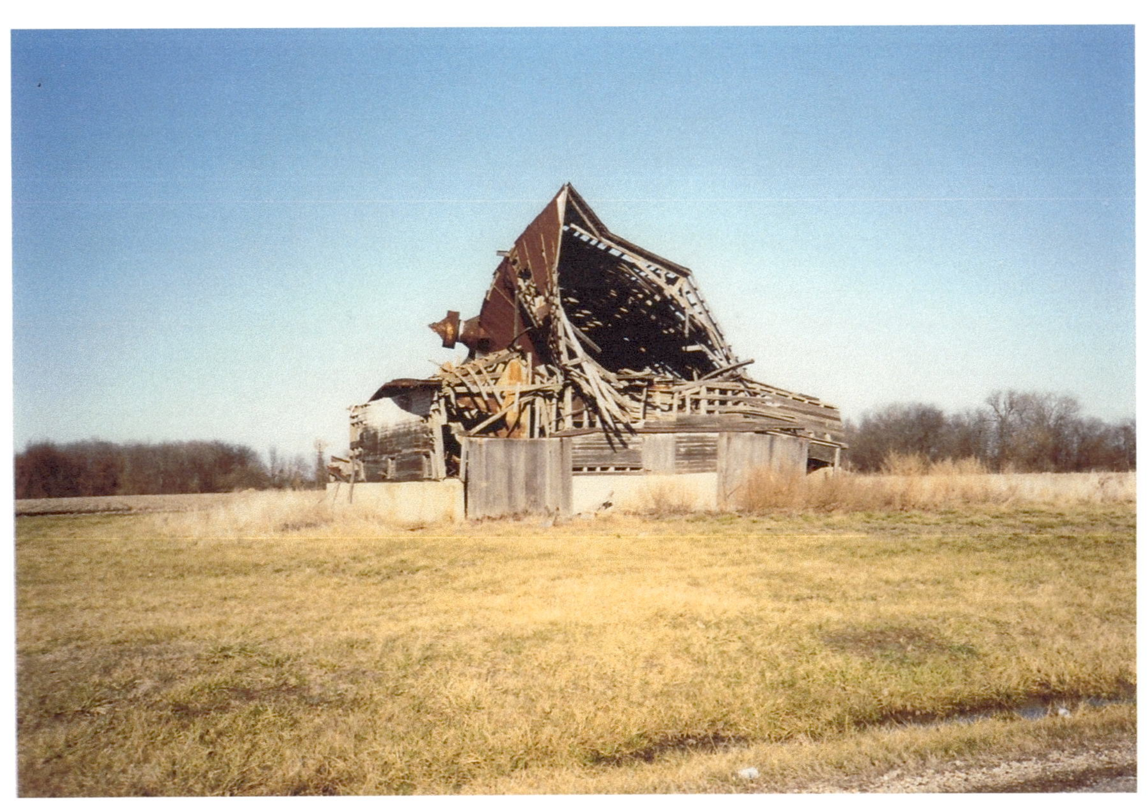

Yet abundant and unceasing

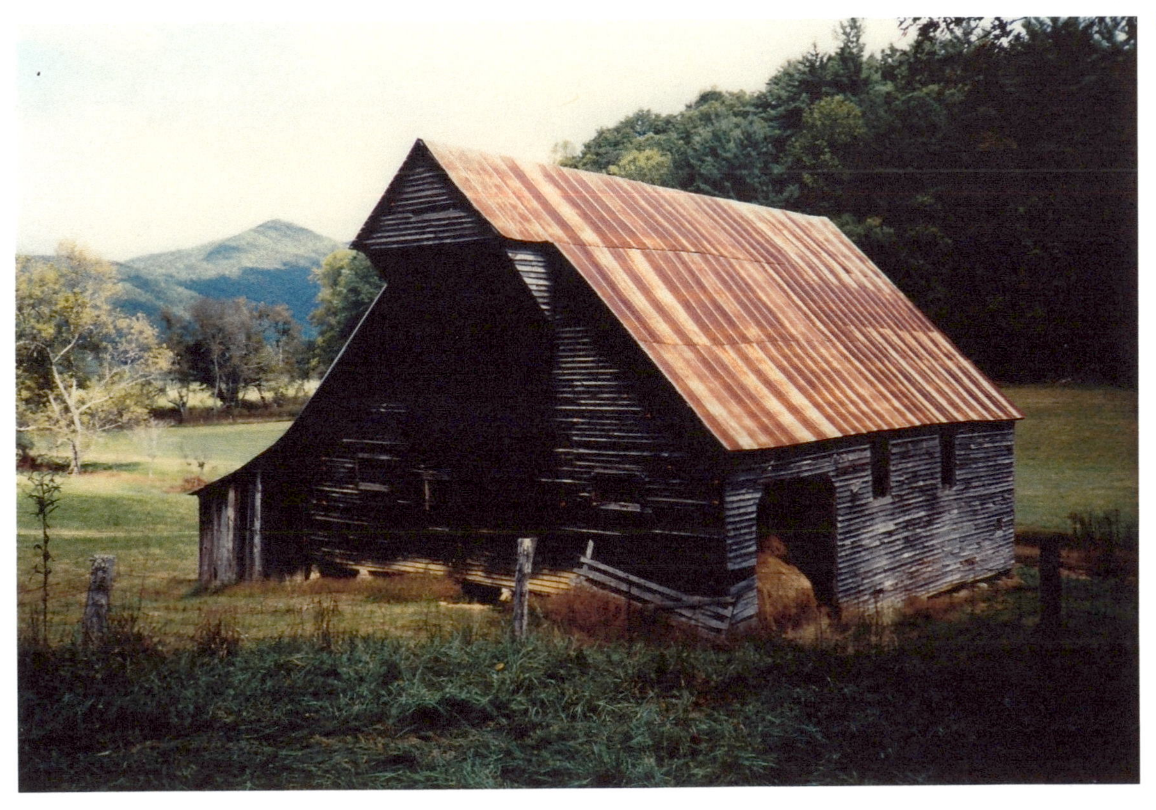

Barn
Smoky Mts.
Tennessee
Oct '86

The harvest of a sower's toil

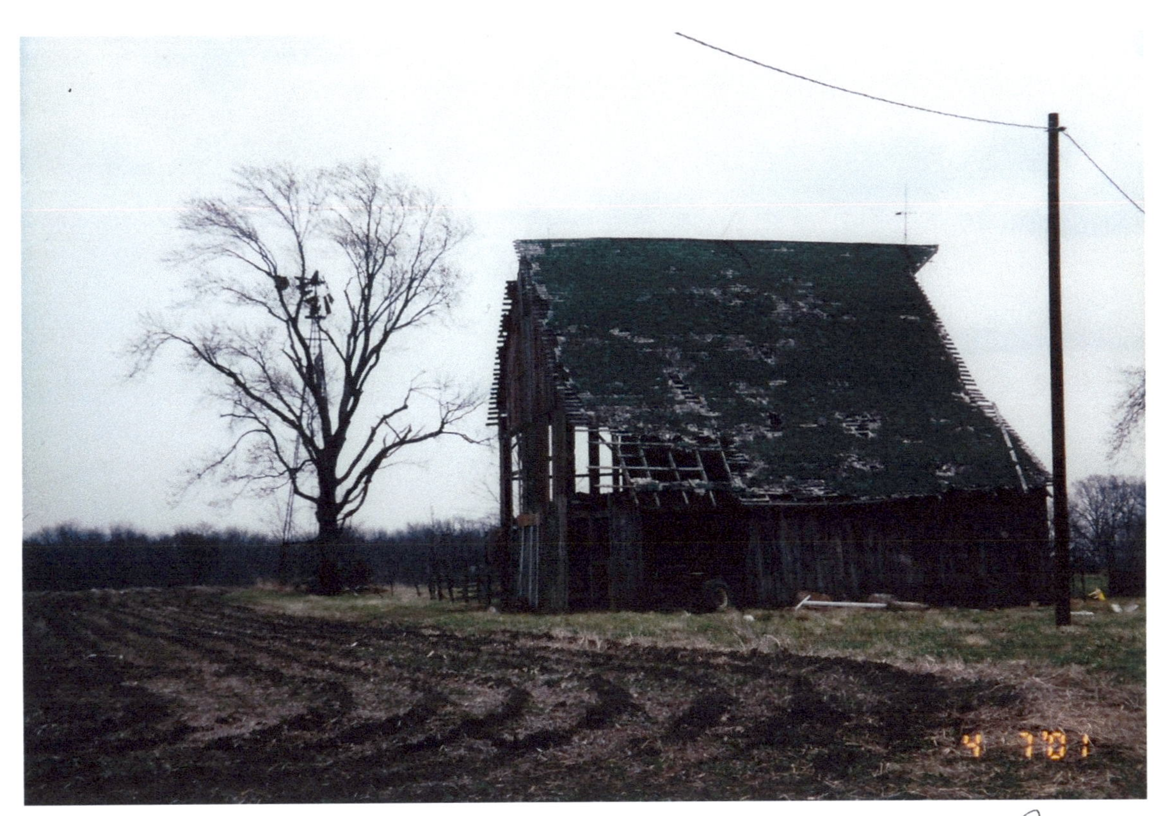

Near Arthur

I am full of life

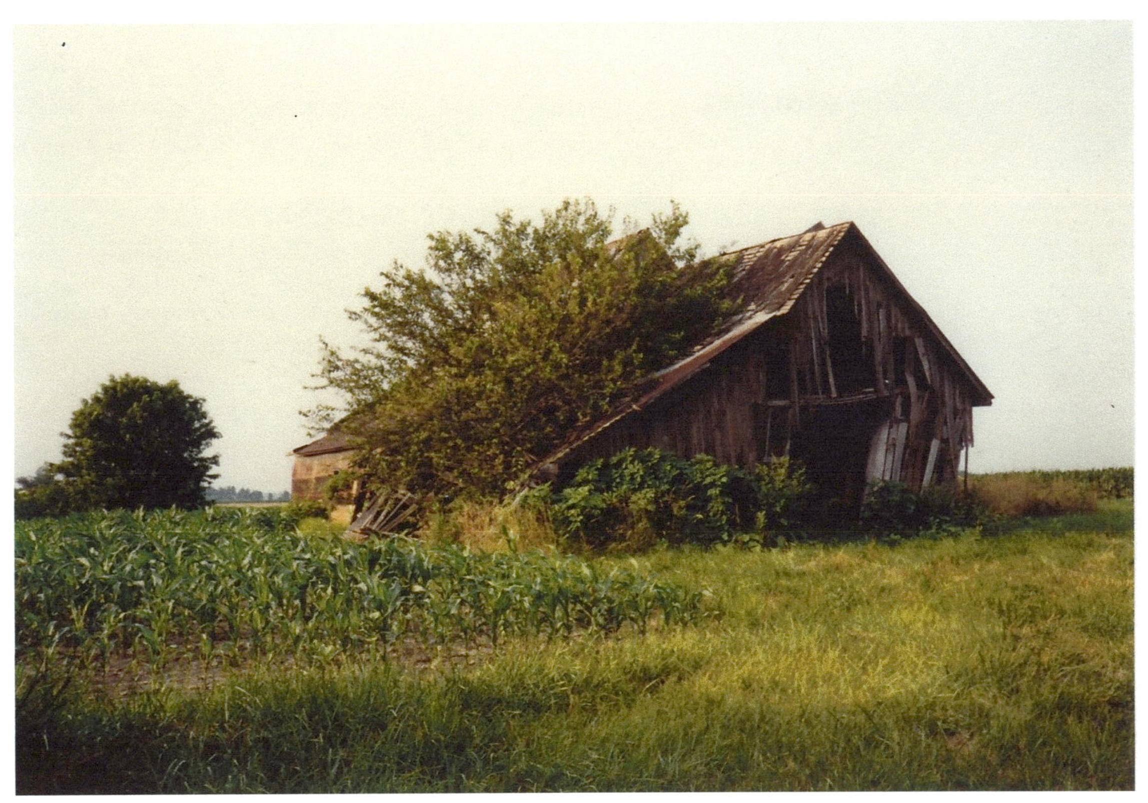

Storing sweet surprises

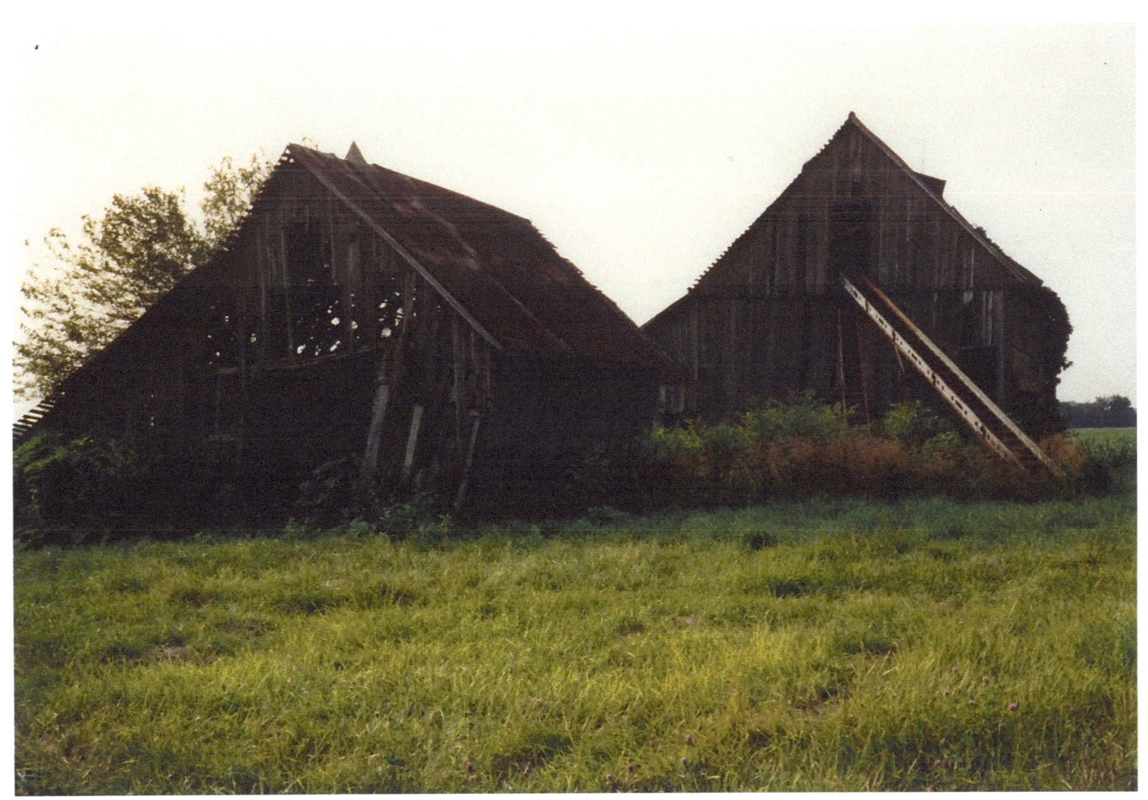

My doors remaining open

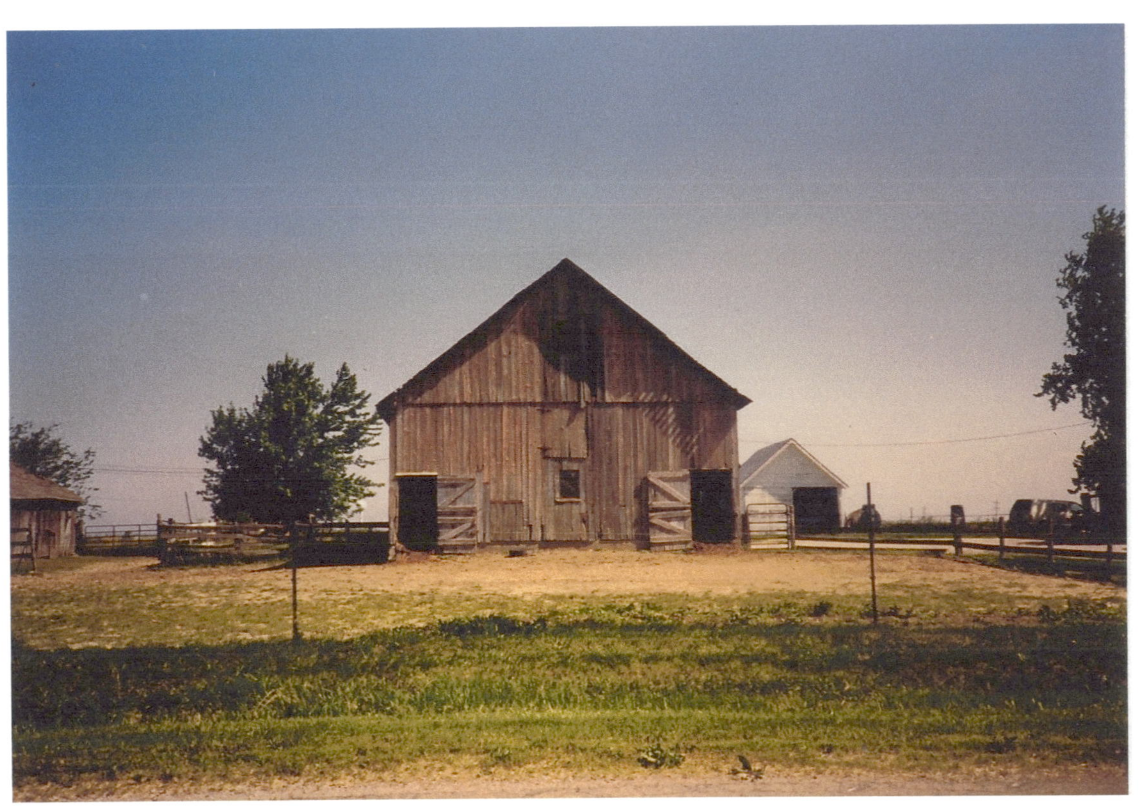

To guests both wild and tame

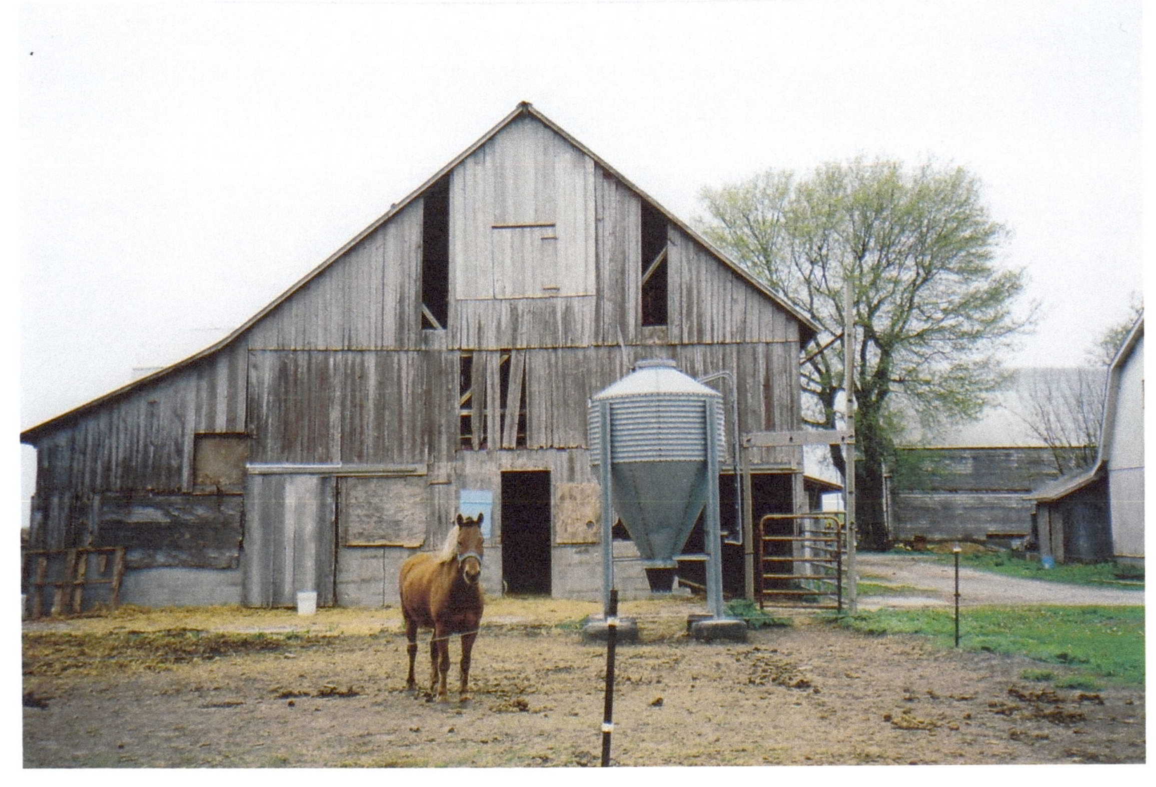

Inveshland
April, 2007

I am always changing

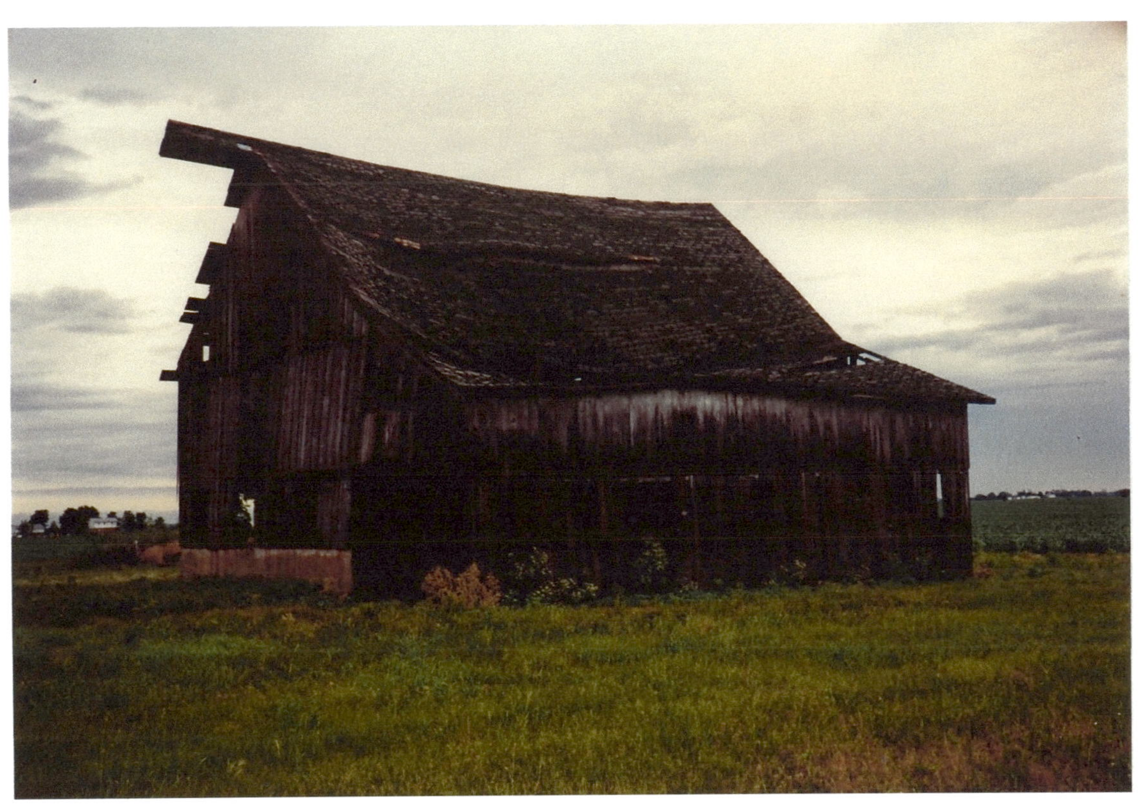

With years of gain and loss

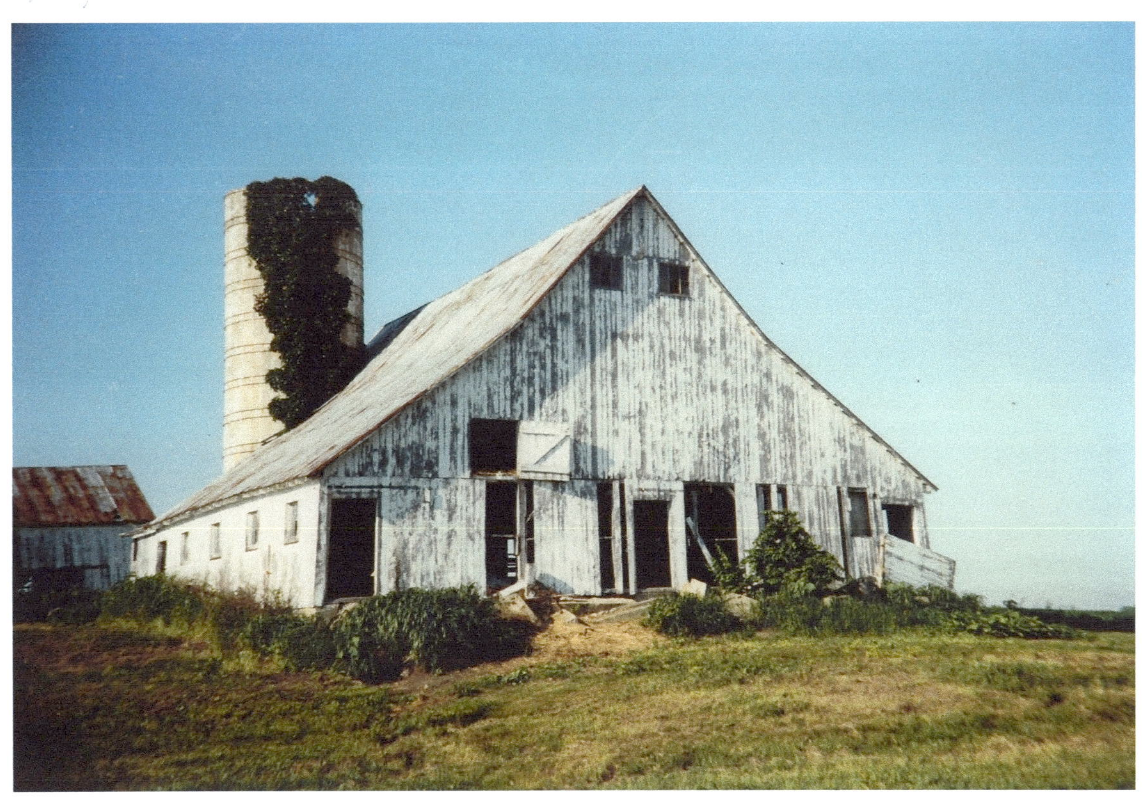
Barn near
Texas ... townsite
Springfield
July '85

While through each passing season

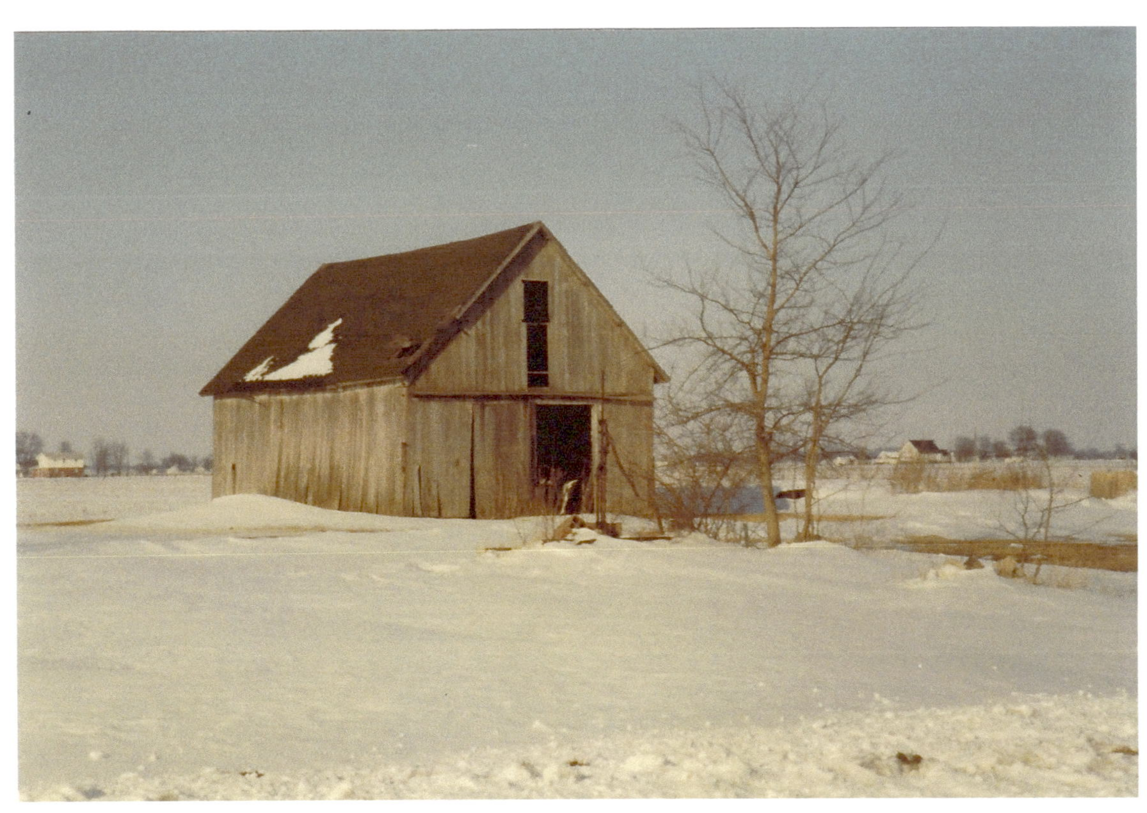

My foundations settle deeper

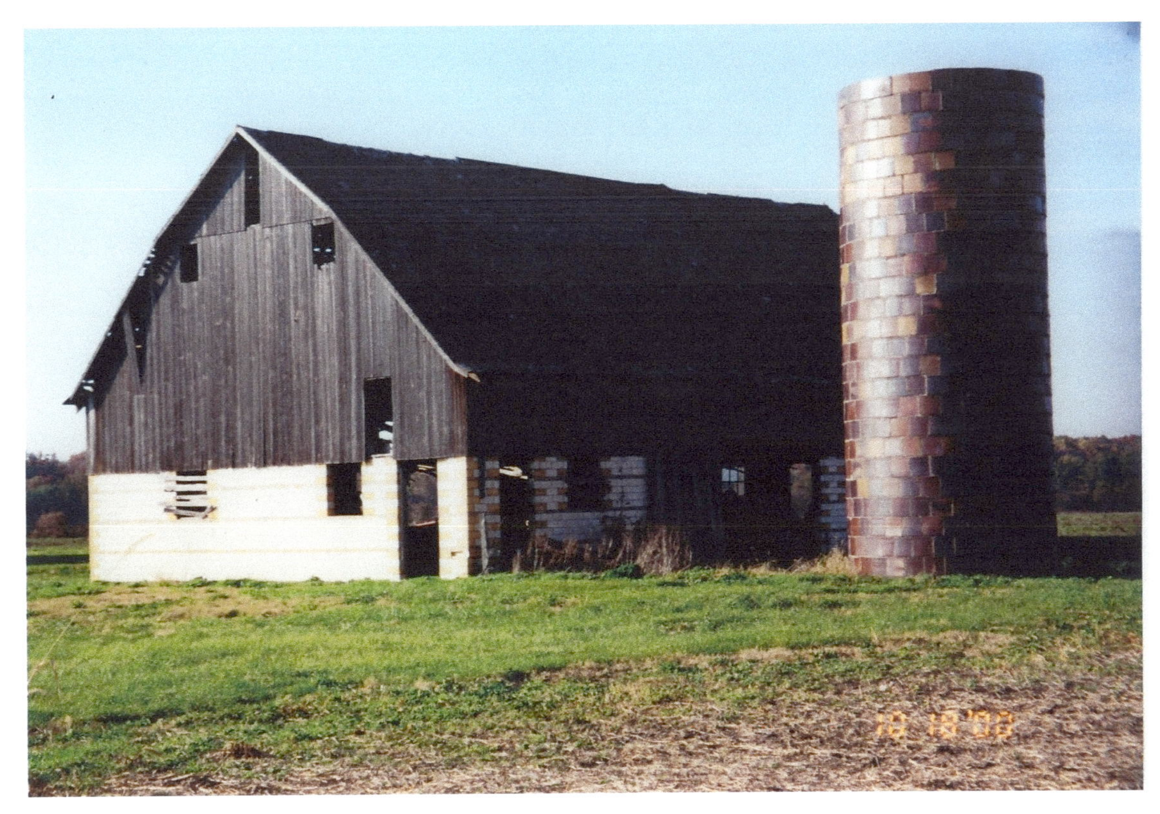
Indiana
Covered Bridge Festival

I am fragile

Amish land

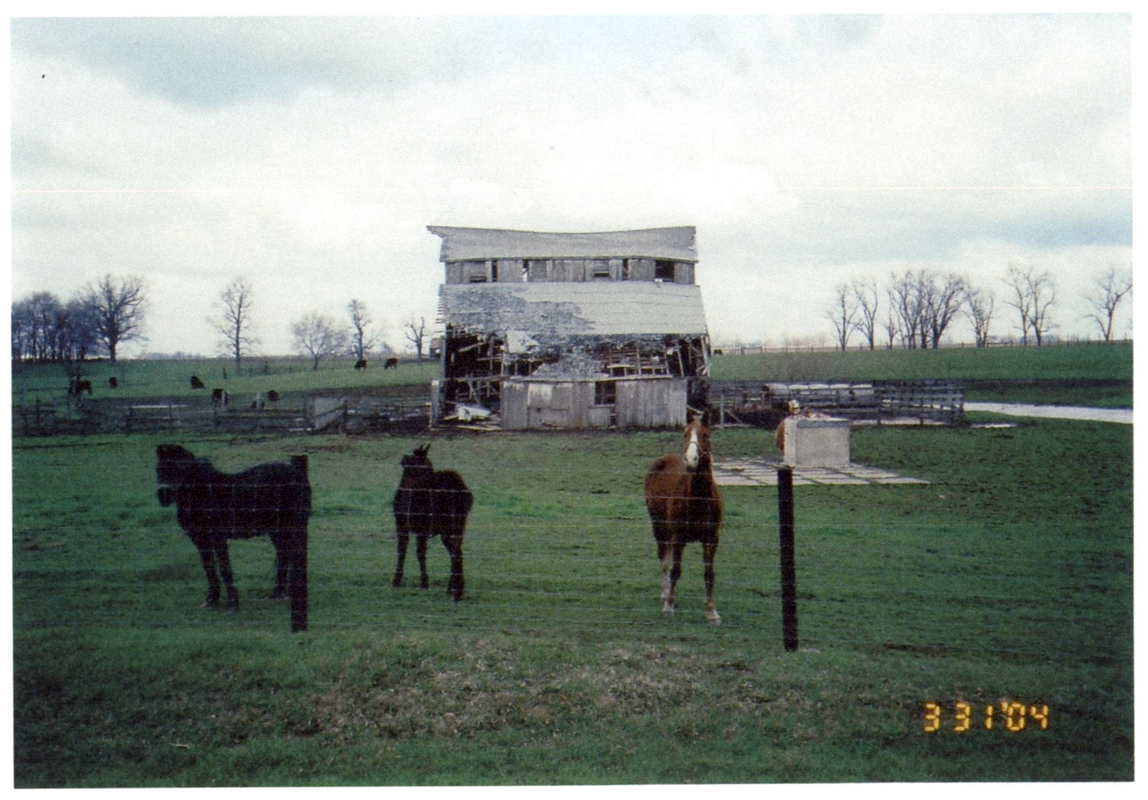

Standing only for a time

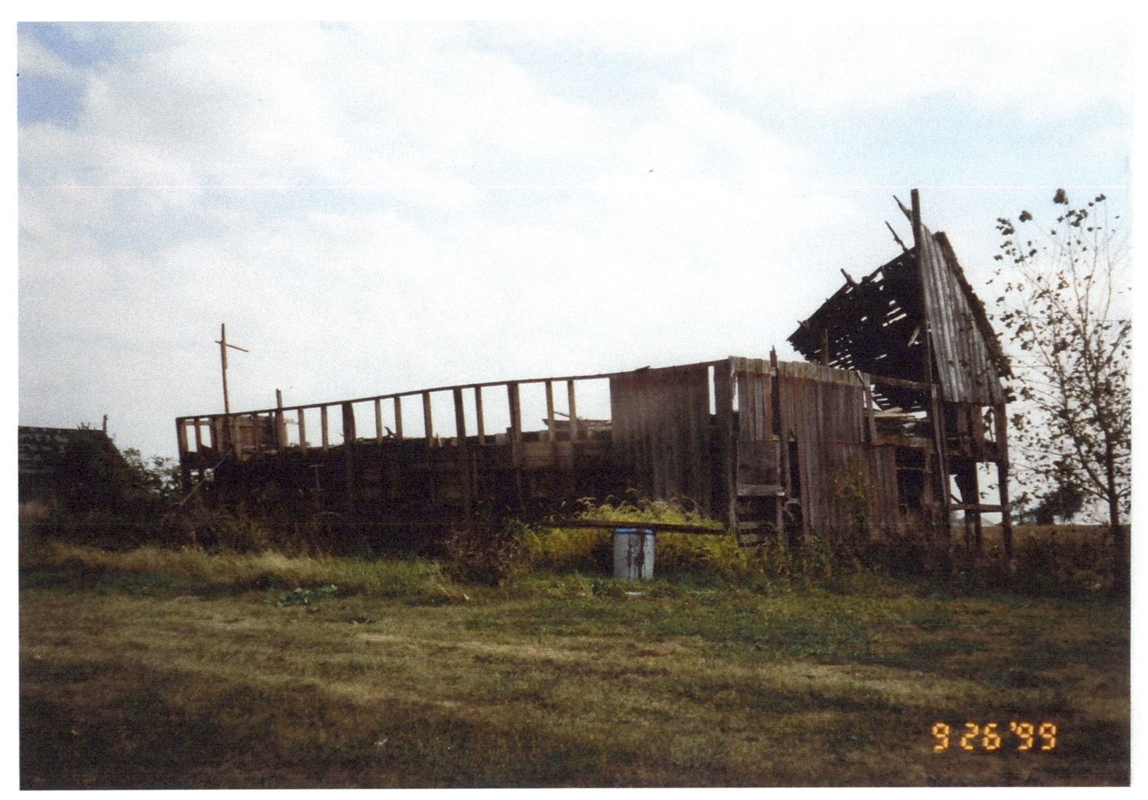

damaged by storm
Laura Dennis' Barn
Washburn

Not always at my best

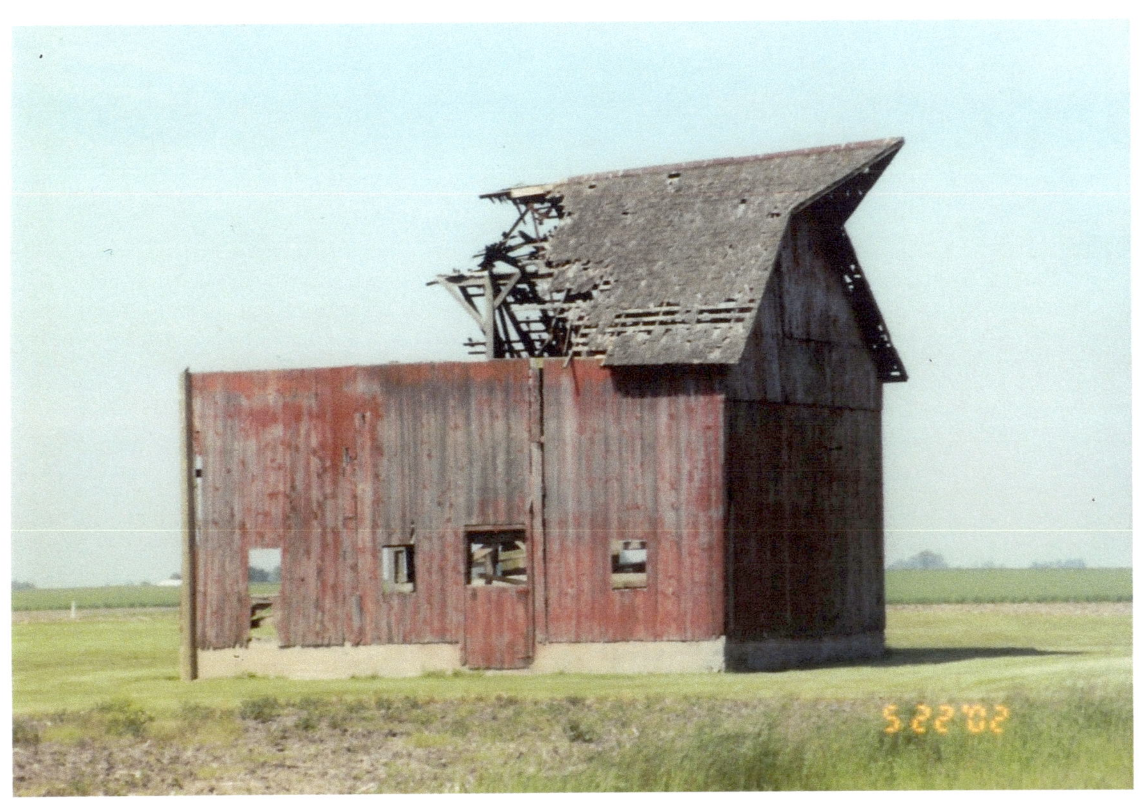

Ameshland

But leaning on strong support

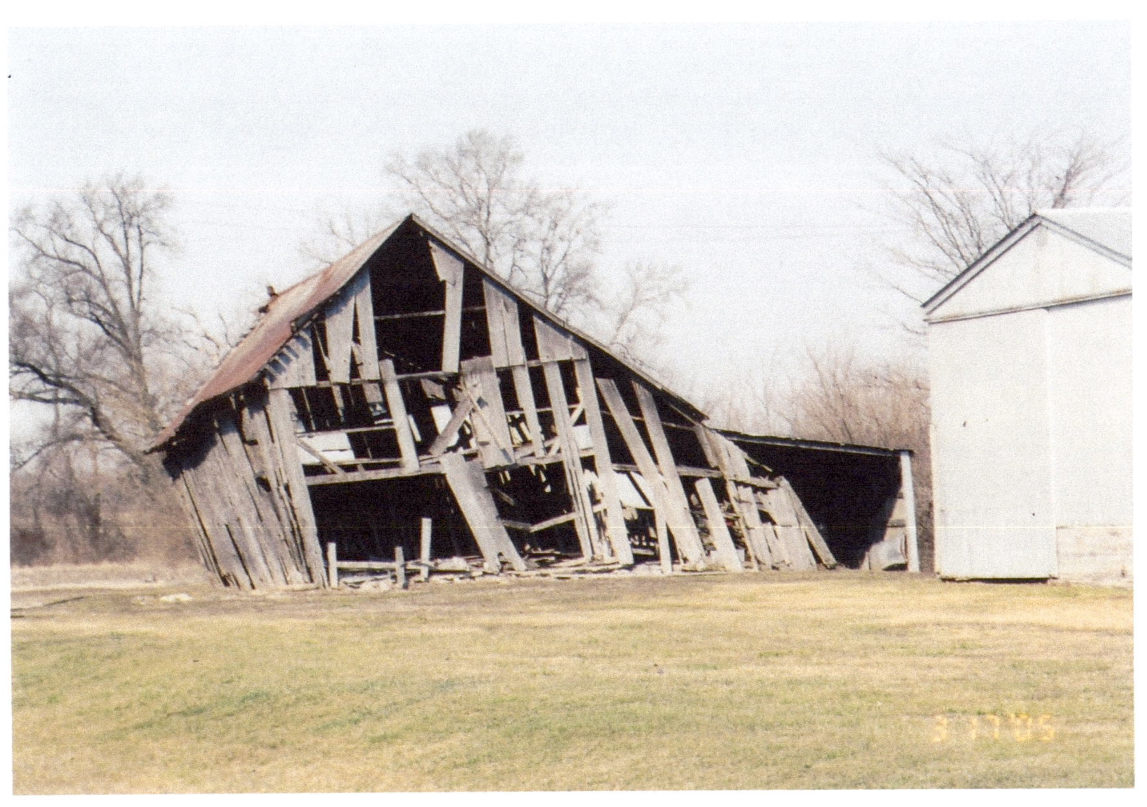

I am remembered

Barn on Interstate between
Champaign & Bloomington
March '85

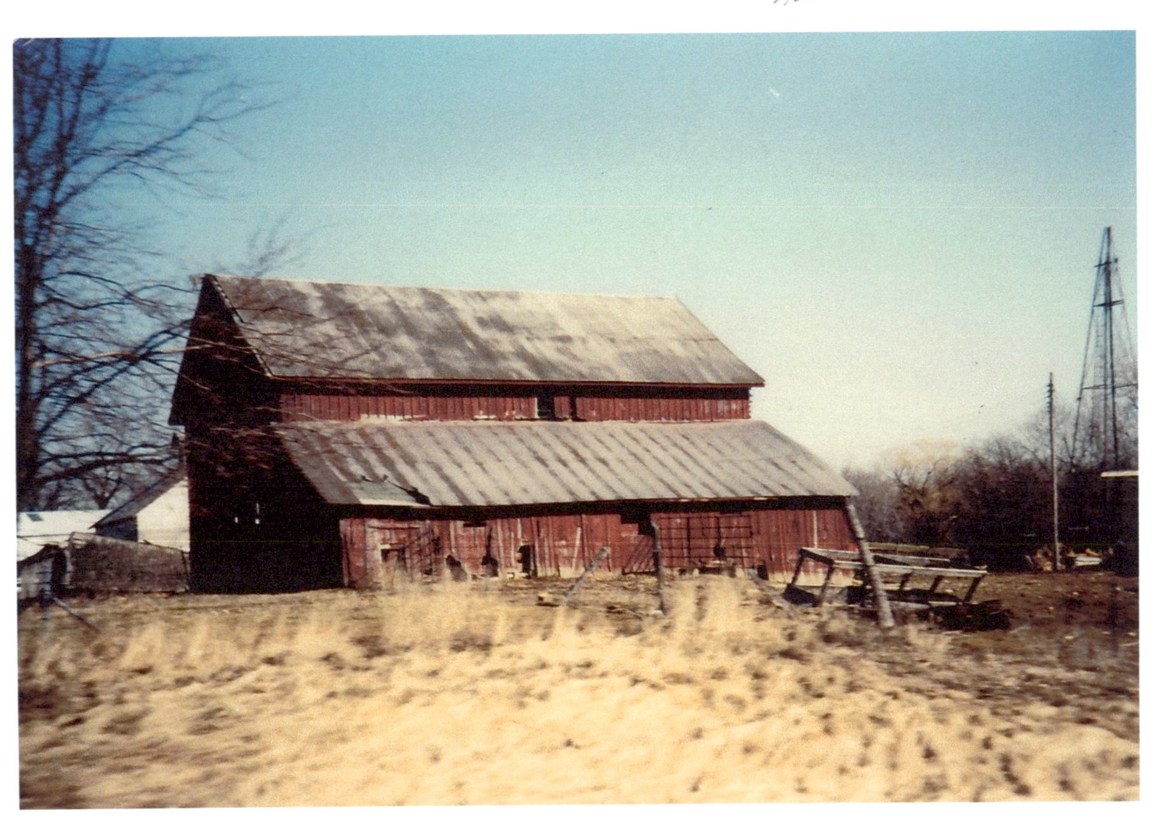

Preserved in heart and time

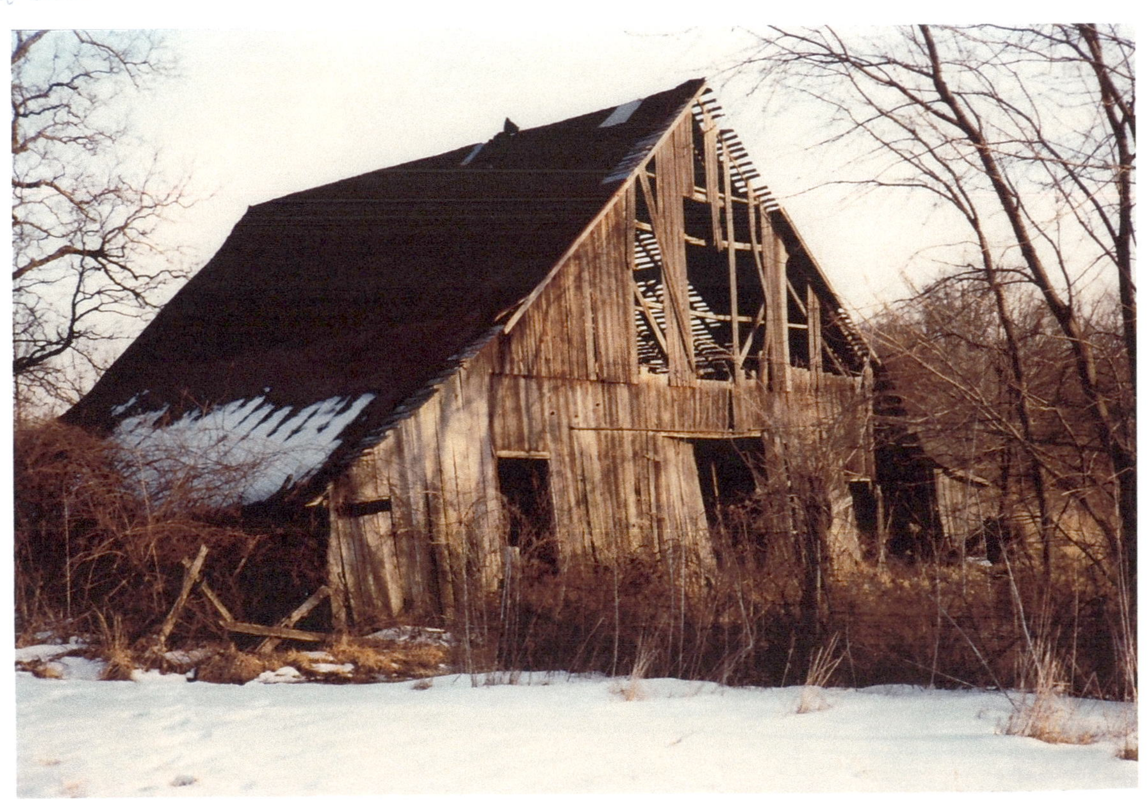

Not alone nor invisible

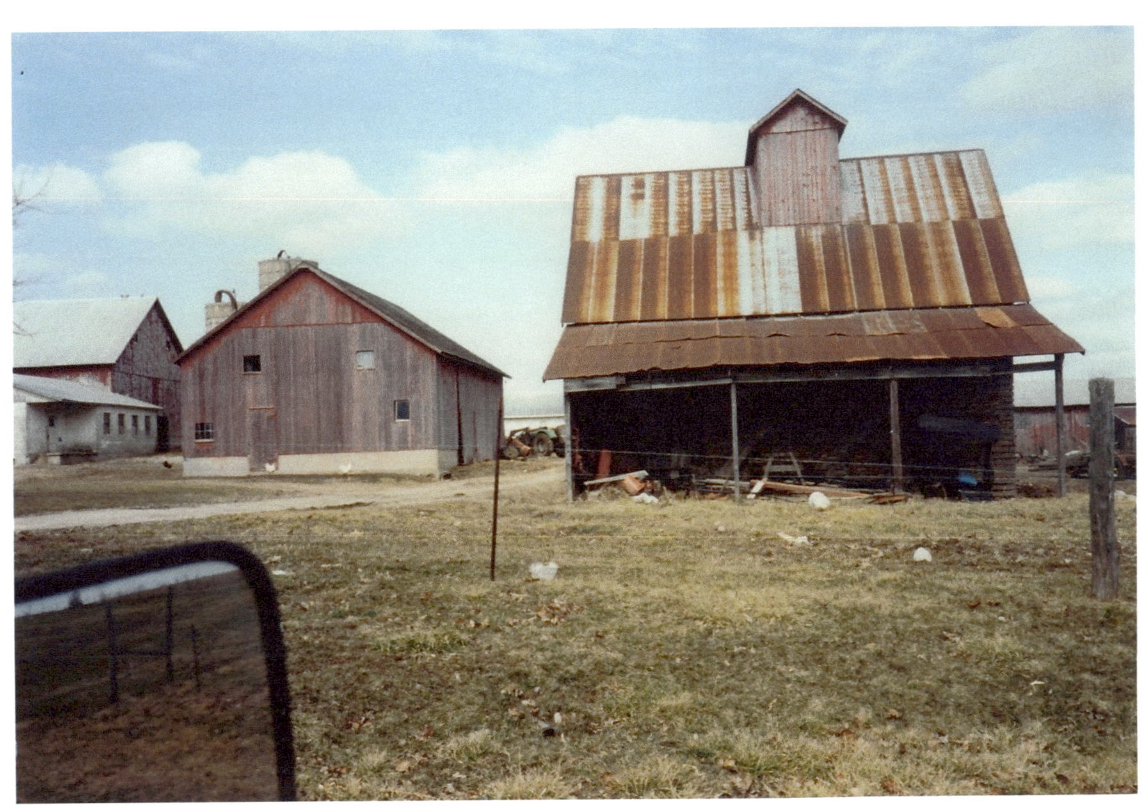

Arthur Hill
March '95

Neither neglected nor replaced

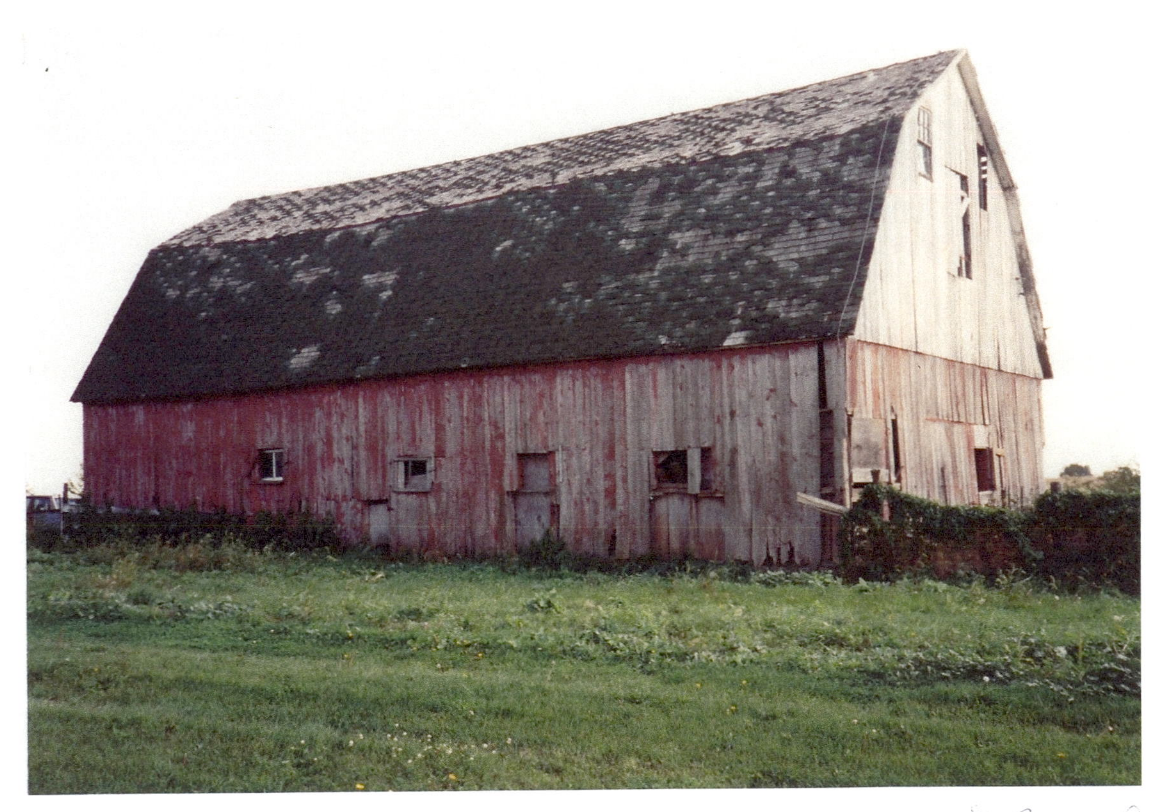
Near Arthur
Oct 1994

I am present even now

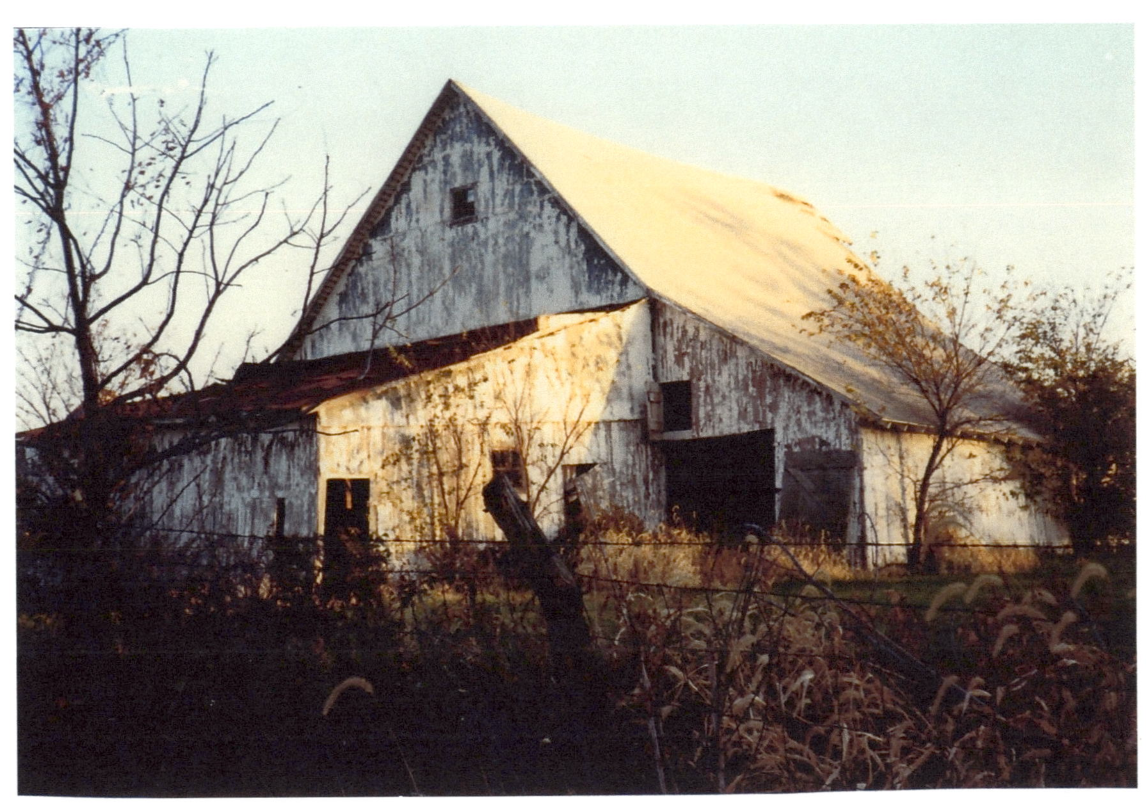

Captured in moments and memories

Nappanee, Ind.
Oct. 1992

The life we made continuing

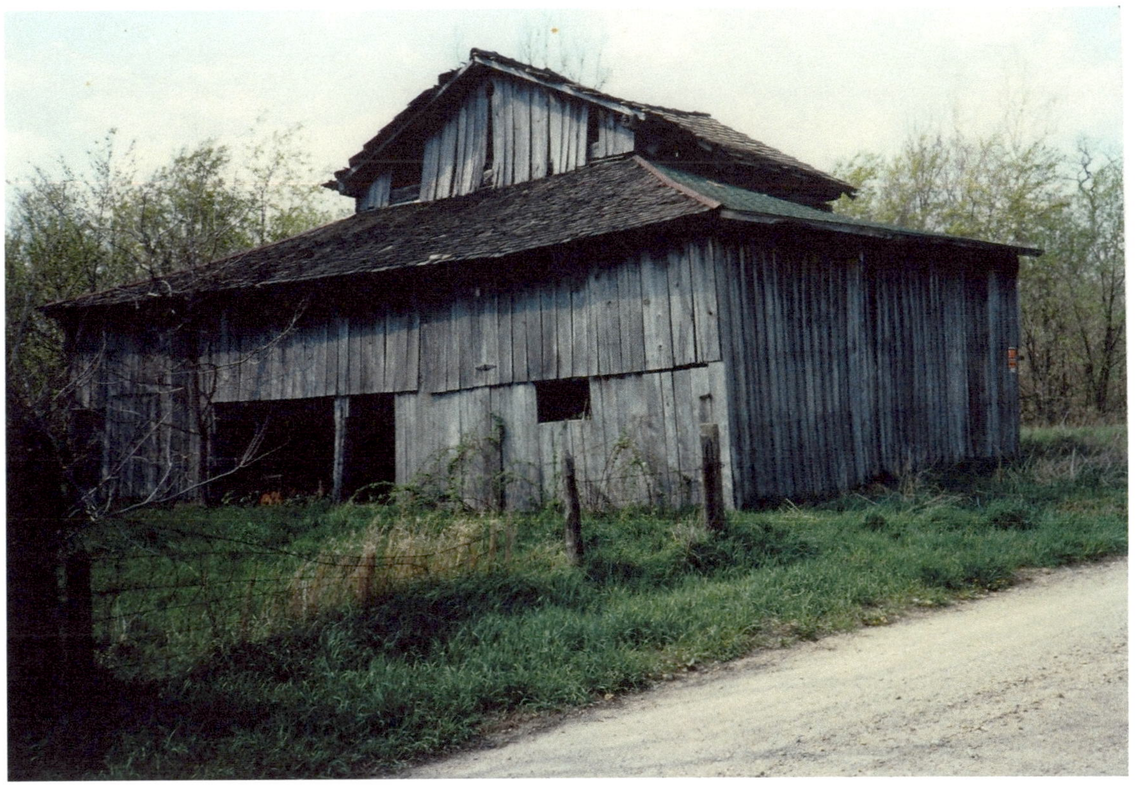

For generations still to come

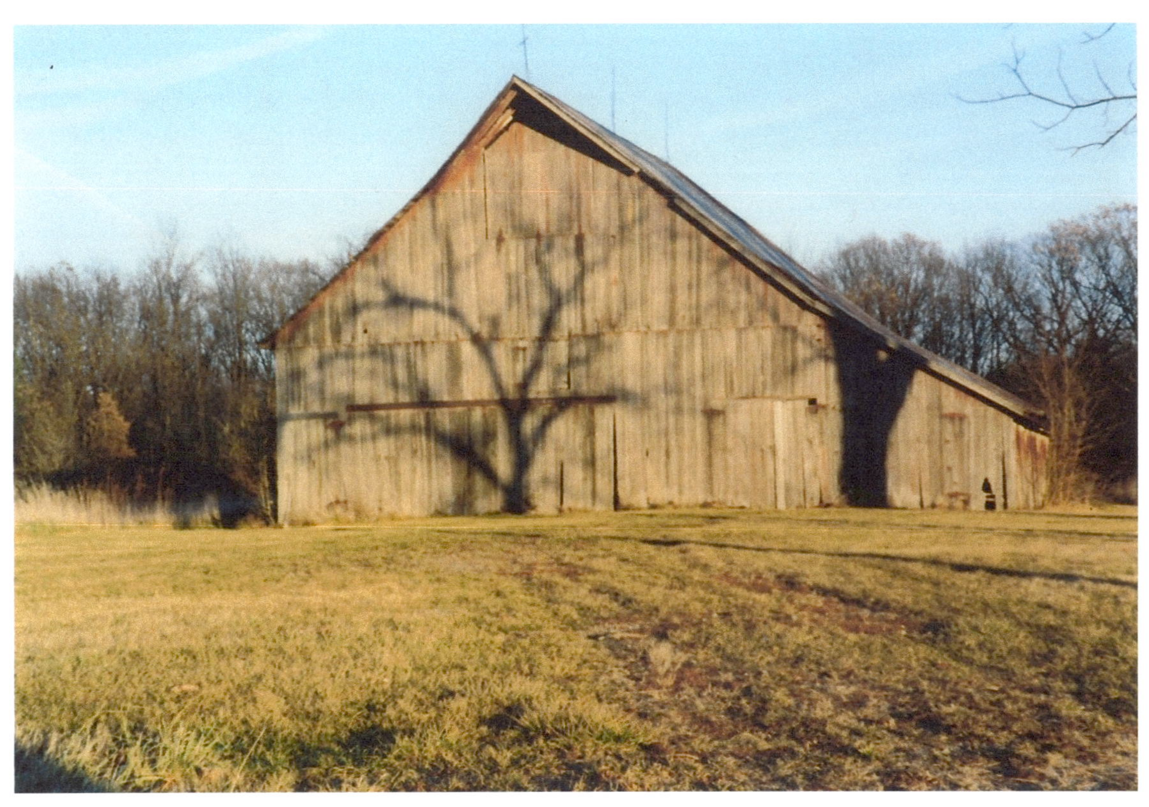

I am treasured

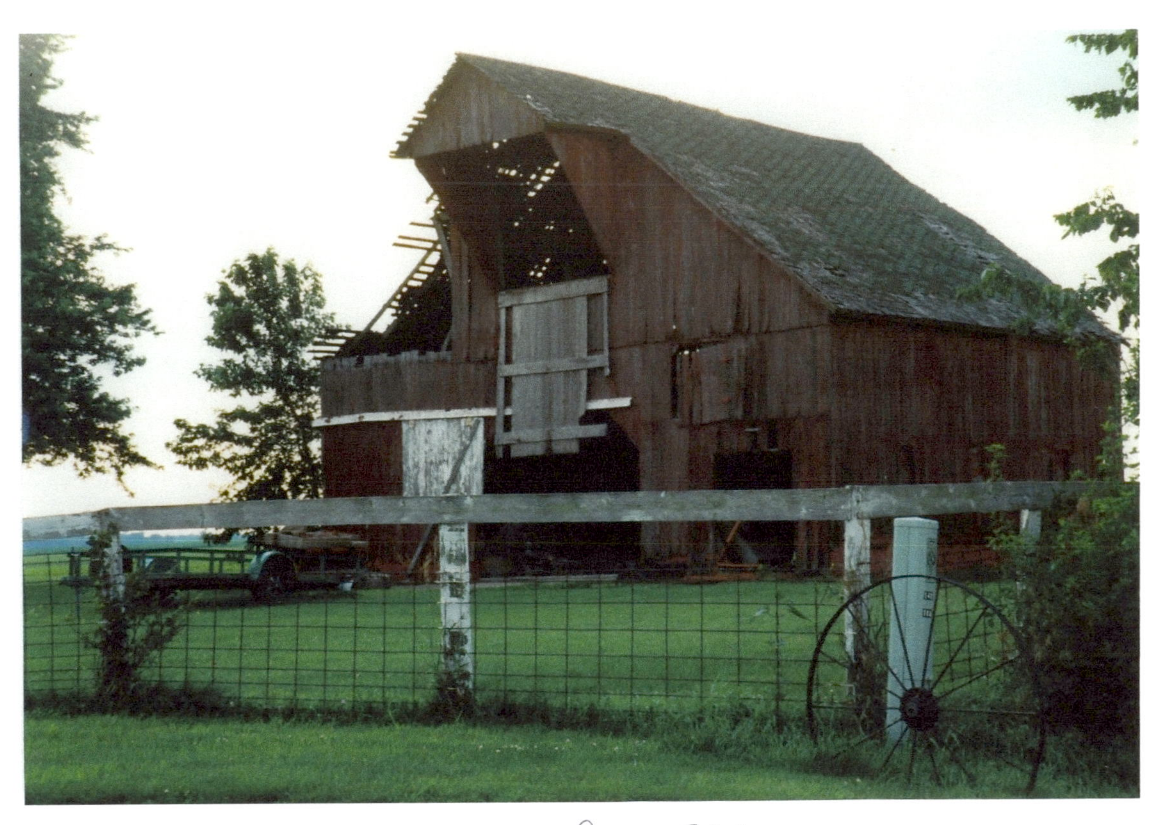

Between Lerna & Toledo

June '98

Now and forever

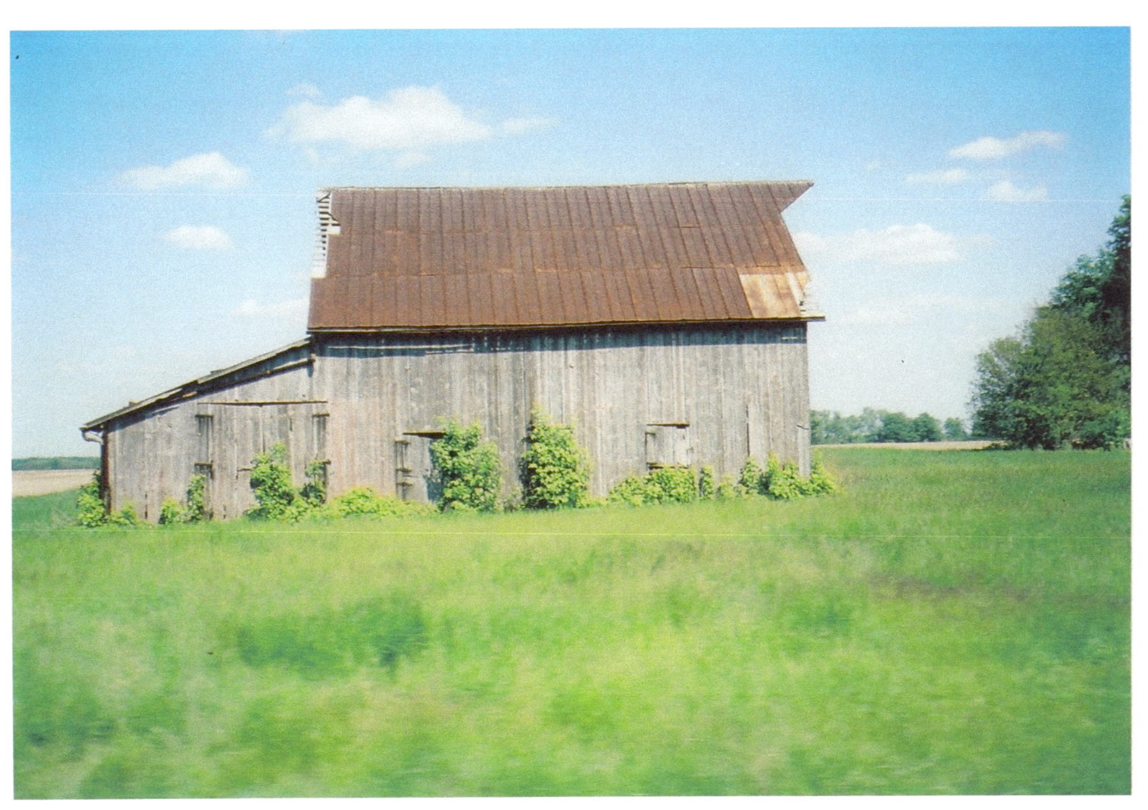

A masterpiece

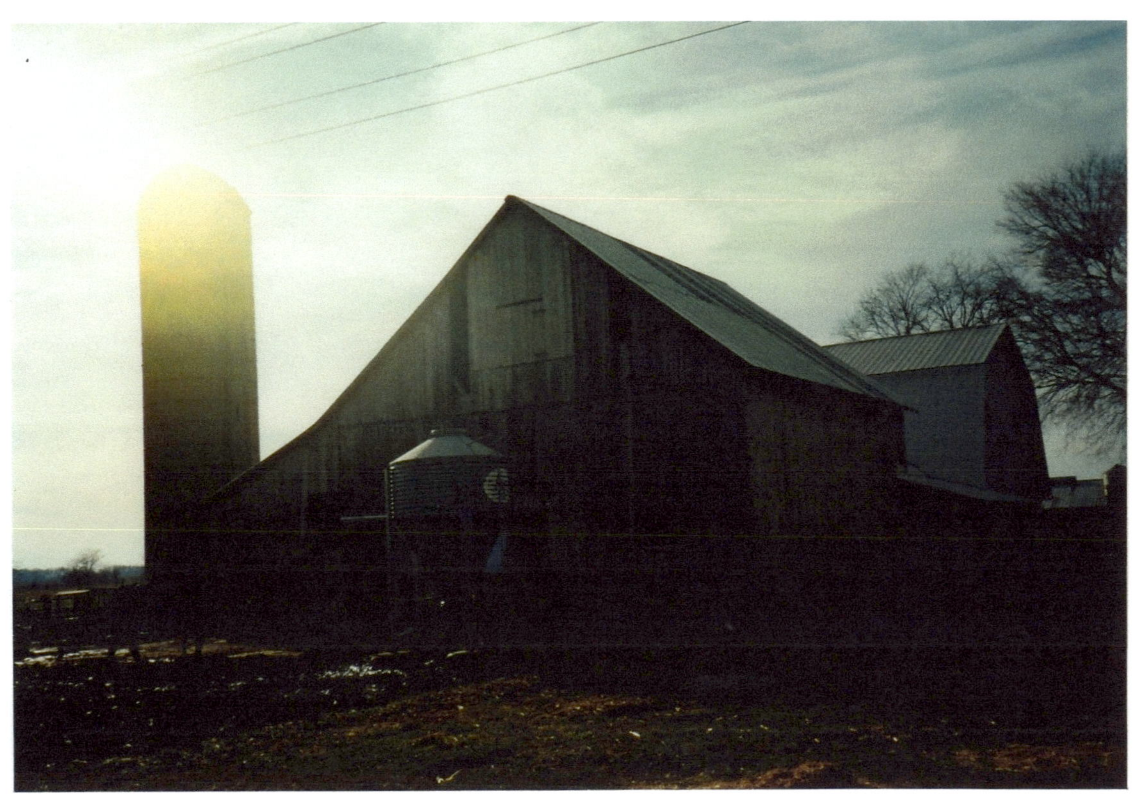

Being held by loving hands

Between Lerna & Toledo, Il.

June '98

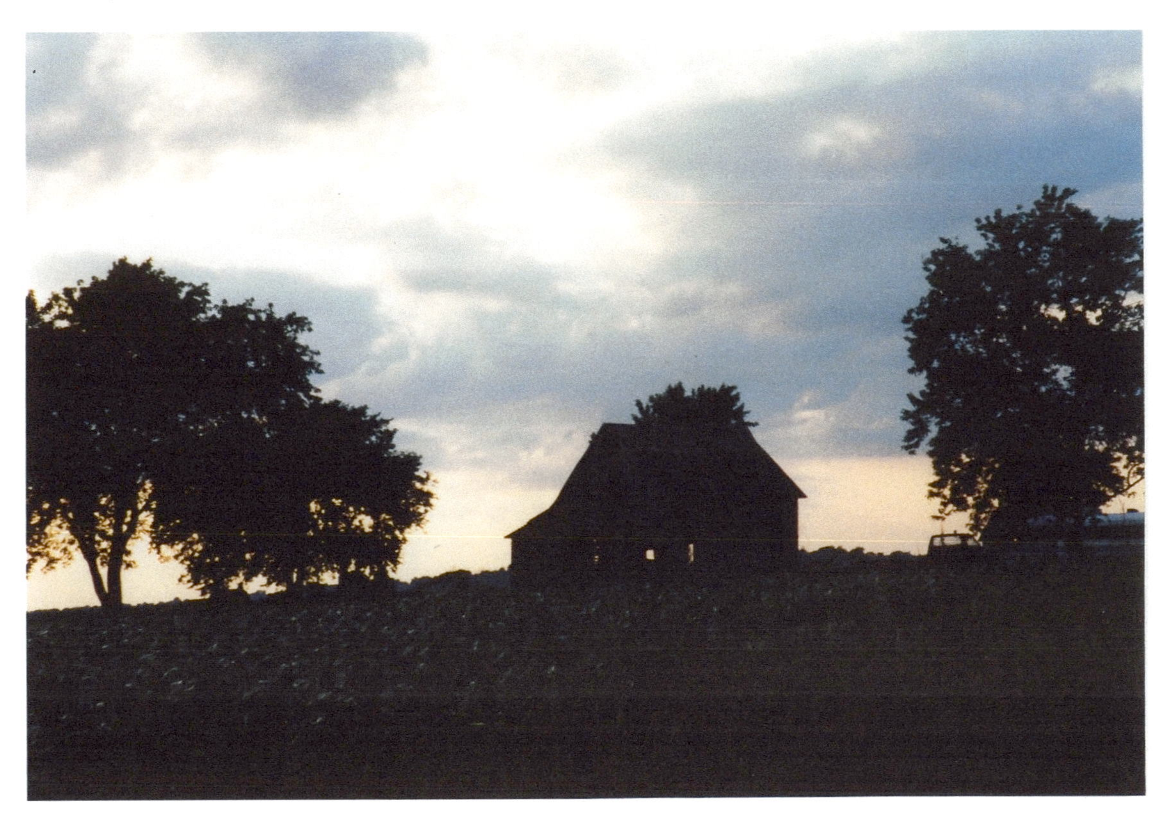

Marilyn Brummet kept her photos meticulously organized in albums
or envelopes, and usually in chronological order. Many of the prints
included in this collection had handwritten notes on them specifying
the date and (sometimes relative) location they were taken.

To preserve her intent and provide a glimpse of insight into her travels
and style, those notes were included alongside each photo exactly as
they were found.

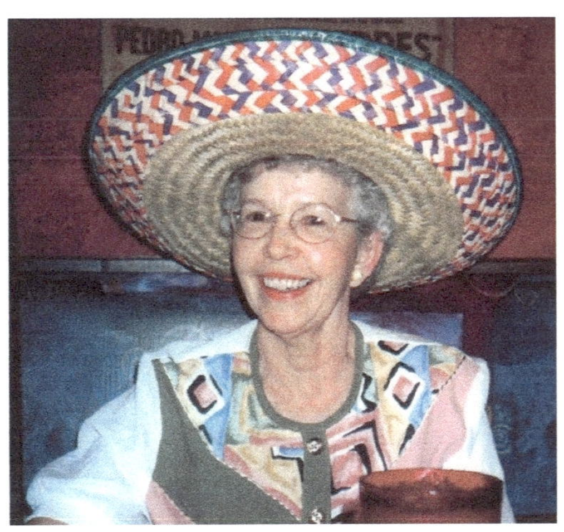

Marilyn Brummet was a nurse,
photographer, mother, grandmother,
and nature enthusiast who lived most
of her life in and around Washburn
and Mattoon, Illinois.

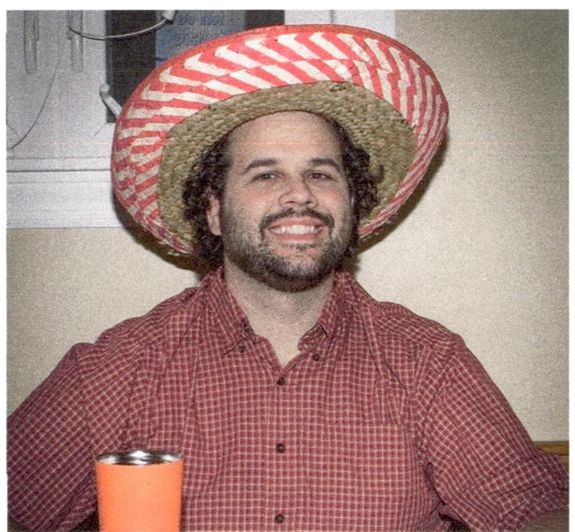

Aaron Brummet is a writer,
editor, son, grandson, and baseball
enthusiast who has lived most of his
life in and around St. Louis,
Missouri and Chicago, Illinois.